Insight Study G

Catriona Mills

WITHDRAWN

No longer the property of the
Boston Public Library.
Sale of this material benefits the Library.

To Kill a Mockingbird

Harper Lee

insight

insight

Harper Lee's To Kill a Mockingbird by Catriona Mills
Insight Study Guide series

Copyright © 2011 Insight Publications Pty Ltd

First published in 2010,
reprinted 2010 by
Insight Publications Pty Ltd
ABN 57 005 102 983
89 Wellington Street
St Kilda VIC 3182
Australia
Tel: +61 3 9523 0044
Fax: +61 3 9523 2044
Email: books@insightpublications.com
Website: www.insightpublications.com

This edition published 2011 in the United States of America by
Insight Publications Pty Ltd, Australia.

ISBN-13: 978-1-921411-68-7

All rights reserved. Except as permitted under U.S. Copyright Act of 1976,
no part of this publication may be reproduced, distributed, or transmitted in any
form or by any means, or stored in a database or retrieval system, without the
prior written permission of the publisher.

Library of Congress Control Number: 2011931355

Cover Design by The Modern Art Production Group
Cover Illustrations by The Modern Art Production Group,
istockphoto® and House Industries
Internal Design by Sarn Potter

Printed in the United States of America by Lightning Source
10 9 8 7 6 5 4 3 2 1

contents

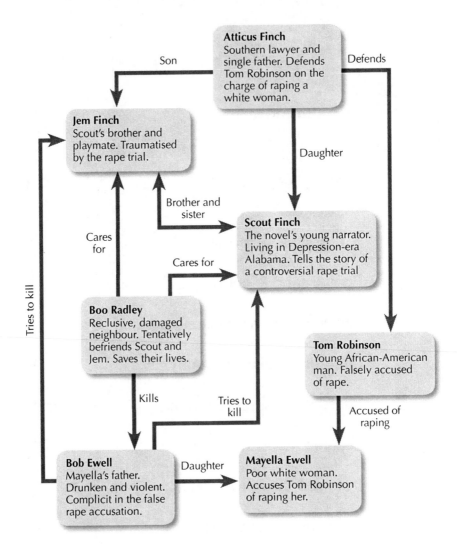

CHARACTER MAP

Atticus Finch
Southern lawyer and single father. Defends Tom Robinson on the charge of raping a white woman.

Son

Defends

Jem Finch
Scout's brother and playmate. Traumatised by the rape trial.

Daughter

Brother and sister

Cares for

Cares for

Scout Finch
The novel's young narrator. Living in Depression-era Alabama. Tells the story of a controversial rape trial

Tries to kill

Boo Radley
Reclusive, damaged neighbour. Tentatively befriends Scout and Jem. Saves their lives.

Tom Robinson
Young African-American man. Falsely accused of rape.

Kills

Tries to kill

Accused of raping

Bob Ewell
Mayella's father. Drunken and violent. Complicit in the false rape accusation.

Daughter

Mayella Ewell
Poor white woman. Accuses Tom Robinson of raping her.

OVERVIEW

About the author

Nelle Harper Lee was born on 28 April 1926 in Monroeville, the county seat of Monroe County, Alabama. She was the third daughter and youngest child of Amasa Coleman ('AC') Lee (a lawyer, member of the Alabama legislature, and partner in the local newspaper) and Frances Cunningham Finch. Despite persistent rumours, the family is not related to the Civil War Confederate general Robert E. Lee.

Lee was a tomboy as a child, socialising largely with her brother Edwin and her friend, the author Truman Capote. Many critics have drawn parallels between Harper Lee and Scout Finch. Biographer Charles J Shields goes further, linking almost every event in the early part of the novel to an event in Lee's life (Shields 2007), though such an approach runs the risk of ignoring the fact that *To Kill a Mockingbird* is ultimately a novel.

Lee attended Monroe County High School, graduating in 1944. The same year, she enrolled in Huntingdon College in Montgomery, Alabama, studying pre-law. (The elder of her two sisters, Alice Lee, was a lawyer.) After her first year, she transferred to the University of Alabama at Tuscaloosa. There she wrote for the humour magazine *Rammer Jammer*, becoming editor-in-chief for 1946–7. She spent the summer of 1948 on student exchange at Oxford University, England, but dropped out of law school on her return.

In 1948, Lee moved to New York to pursue a career as a writer. She worked in low-paying jobs (such as bookstore clerk and airline-ticket seller) while trying to write sufficient material to send to an agent. Finally, in 1957, she sent the manuscript of *To Kill a Mockingbird* (then called *Atticus*) to publisher Jonathan Lippincott. Lee worked closely with an editor for nearly two years, preparing the novel for publication.

To Kill a Mockingbird was published in 1960, and in 1961 won the Pulitzer Prize for Fiction, a distinguished award for fiction by an American author, preferably on a facet of American life. In 1962, the film adaptation was released. Lee has published only a small number of short works since *To Kill a Mockingbird*, though she did work on an unfinished second novel, *The Long Goodbye*.

Harper Lee is often listed, along with the late JD Salinger and Thomas Pynchon, as one of the most famously reclusive American authors, just as Boo Radley is one of literature's most famous recluses. Pynchon himself once said (via telephone) that 'My belief is that "recluse" is a codeword generated by journalists, meaning "doesn't like to talk to reporters"'. Lee has rarely made public appearances or granted interviews since the mid-1960s. After her literary career largely stopped with her first novel, she has kept her private life private. As a result, biographical material on Lee is rare. The only full-length biography written for adults (several have been written for young adults) is Charles J Shields' *Mockingbird: A Portrait of Harper Lee* (2007). Though Shields' biography is based on hundreds of interviews with friends and colleagues and makes extensive use of secondary sources, it must be read cautiously, as Lee herself refused to participate in the process.

Synopsis

Narrated by the six-year-old Scout, *To Kill a Mockingbird* traces two years in the life of Scout and Jem Finch, growing up in the Depression-era Deep South. In the opening chapters, Scout covers their early life in the small town of Maycomb, Alabama, including her early experiences of school and friendship with Charles Baker ('Dill') Harris, who visits every summer. During this time, she and Jem become obsessed with their mysterious neighbour, Boo Radley, a man who has been imprisoned at home by his family after youthful misdemeanours. Although the children at first see him as a malevolent phantom, he makes a series of friendly overtures towards them, such as leaving them small presents.

Two years after the novel begins, the children become aware that their father, Atticus, a local lawyer, is being criticised for his decision to defend an African-American man, Tom Robinson, on the charge of raping a white woman, Mayella Ewell. As the trial approaches, tensions in the town increase, including an attempt to remove Tom from the jail to lynch him the night before his trial.

The trial testimonies of Mayella Ewell and her father, Bob, show flaws in their version of events, while Tom's testimony, which presents him as a kind and sensitive man, reveals that Bob sexually and physically abuses his daughter. Nevertheless, Tom is convicted and sentenced to death. While Atticus prepares an appeal, Tom attempts to escape from jail and is shot dead by the guards.

After Tom's death, the town slowly forgets the trial, except for Jem, who is tormented by the injustice of the sentence, and Bob Ewell, who harasses Tom's widow Helen, the trial judge and Atticus. On the evening of the Halloween pageant at the school, Bob Ewell attacks Jem and Scout, breaking Jem's arm. He is stabbed to death by Boo Radley, and the town's authorities, in the form of Atticus and Heck Tate, decide to tell the town that the death was accidental.

Character summaries

Scout Finch: Atticus' daughter and Jem's sister; nearly six years old at the beginning of the novel; the novel's narrator.

Jem Finch: Atticus' son and Scout's elder brother; nearly ten years old at the beginning of the novel; the novel purports to tell the story of how he broke his arm.

Atticus Finch: Father to Scout and Jem; fifty-year-old widower; local lawyer and state legislator; defends Tom Robinson on the charge of raping a white woman.

Dill Harris: Friend to Scout and Jem, and nephew of their neighbour Miss Rachel; nearly seven years old at the beginning of the novel; inspires Scout and Jem's fascination with Boo Radley.

Tom Robinson: Twenty-five-year-old African-American man; married with three children; works as a cotton picker; accused of raping Mayella Ewell.

Calpurnia: African-American housekeeper for Atticus and his family; around fifty years old, with grown children; acts as a female authority figure for Scout and Jem.

Bob Ewell: Middle-aged unemployed and alcoholic man on the outskirts of Maycomb society; widower and father of a large family; accuses Tom Robinson of raping his daughter Mayella.

Mayella Ewell: Nineteen-year-old daughter of Bob Ewell; subjected to her father's abuse; accuses Tom Robinson of rape.

Boo Radley: Middle-aged neighbour to the Finches; imprisoned in his own home by his family; terrifies Scout and Jem until they slowly build a relationship with him.

Miss Maudie: Middle-aged neighbour to the Finches; widowed; provides guidance to Scout and Jem.

Aunt Alexandra: Atticus' sister; married and living on the family property; comes to live with Atticus to provide Scout with a feminine influence.

BACKGROUND & CONTEXT

To understand the context of *To Kill a Mockingbird*, the reader needs to consider two significant time periods: 1933–5, when the novel is set, and the late 1950s, when Lee was writing it. (Note: in this guide 'southern' refers to geography; 'Southern' is used to refer to the culture of the American South.)

Racism and the Great Depression: Alabama in the 1930s

> They used to tell me I was building a dream,
> and so I followed the mob,
> When there was earth to plow, or guns to bear,
> I was always there right on the job.
> They used to tell me I was building a dream,
> with peace and glory ahead,
> Why should I be standing in line, just waiting for bread?

> From 'Brother, Can You Spare a Dime?,'
> lyrics by EY 'Yip' Harburg (1931)

Between 1861 and 1865, the American Civil war was fought between the northern states (states in which the slavery of African-Americans was illegal) and the southern states (states in which slavery was legal), after eleven of the southern states seceded from the Union in 1860 and 1861 and formed the Confederate States of America (or Confederacy). When the Confederacy surrendered in 1865, slavery was abolished throughout the United States via the Thirteenth Amendment to the United States Constitution. This brought an end to formalised slavery, but not to the division between the northern and southern states or to racial segregation.

By the 1930s, the Civil War was beyond living memory for most people in the South. But it continued to mark a significant point of difference between the North and the South. Southern self-identity remained sharply divided from Northern self-identity (see **Themes, Ideas & Values**) and the war did not bring an end to racial segregation, particularly not in the Deep South.

Between 1876 and 1965, southern states enacted a series of state and local laws known collectively as the 'Jim Crow laws' (named for the 1828 song 'Jump Jim Crow', performed by a white comedian made up to appear African-American). The Jim Crow laws enforced legal segregation between African-Americans and white Americans in all public facilities and spaces, including schools, public transport, restaurants, and prisons. The Jim Crow laws were separate from the Black Codes, also enacted in the South, which denied African-Americans the right to testify against white Americans, serve on juries and in state militias, or vote.

Supporters of segregation maintained that it meant African-Americans were 'separate but equal'. Mrs Merriweather, for example, endorses the laws at the missionary tea late in the novel, when she says,

> People up there set 'em free, but you don't see 'em setting at the table with 'em. At least we don't have the deceit to say to 'em yes you're as good as we are but stay away from us (p.258).

In practice, the laws were an example of systemic, institutionalised racism.

In the 1930s, these problems were compounded by the difficulties of the Great Depression, a worldwide economic depression triggered by the Wall Street Crash of 1929, when share prices on the New York Stock Exchange collapsed and continued to fall for a month. The effects spread out from the US across the world, persisting from 1929 to (in some countries) the early 1940s. Both cities and rural areas were affected: the cities as industry collapsed and the rural areas as crop prices were more than halved. As Atticus notes, 'professional people were poor because the farmers were poor' (p.23). The situation became so desperate that the Depression's early years (1931–5) became known as the 'public enemy era,' when bank robbers such as John Dillinger, Pretty Boy Floyd, Baby Face Nelson, and Bonnie and Clyde (all shot by law enforcement in 1934) became folk heroes to a struggling population.

Racism and the Civil Rights Movement: Alabama in the 1950s

> Southern trees bear strange fruit,
> Blood on the leaves and blood at the root,
> Black body swinging in the Southern breeze,
> Strange fruit hanging from the poplar trees.

> 'Strange Fruit,' lyrics by Abel Meeropol
> (Lewis Allen) (1936)

By the 1950s, when Lee was writing her novel, both the Great Depression and World War II had ended, but the Jim Crow laws were still in effect. It was also a time when both the Civil Rights Movement and the third wave of the Ku Klux Klan were on the rise.

The African-American Civil Rights Movement was devoted to ending legalised segregation and restoring the right to vote in southern states. Though its history reaches back to before the Civil War (as in the case of the Underground Railroad, which helped escaped slaves reach the northern states), the movement became more politicised and powerful after World War II. Alabama was the focus of many significant moments in the Civil Rights Movement: civil rights activist Rosa Parks' refusal to give up her bus seat to a white passenger (Montgomery, 1955); the Montgomery Bus

Boycott, a year-long boycott of public transport in support of Parks, led by Dr Martin Luther King (1955–6); and the later Selma to Montgomery marches, in which state and local police attacked the marchers (1965).

'Ku Klux Klan' refers to several associated far-right, white-supremacist groups that, although they strongly resemble one another, are not a single continuous organisation with an unbroken history. The first Klan was founded in Tennessee (a southern state bordering Alabama) in 1866, after the end of the Civil War. This Klan particularly targeted freedmen (former slaves) and politicians who favoured civil rights: its membership was largely southern. Its activities were curtailed in the 1870s when the US Congress passed a series of Force Acts that specifically targeted Klan behaviour.

The second Klan was founded in Georgia (another southern state, also bordering Alabama) in 1915, the same year in which Jewish-American Leo Frank was lynched in Georgia after being convicted of killing a white teenager. The second wave of the Klan built slowly: Shawn Lay notes that 'the Klan's membership remained small, numbering only a few thousand by the end of 1919, almost all of whom resided in Georgia and Alabama' (Lay 2004, pp. 6–7). After peaking in popularity in the 1920s, this wave decreased in numbers and force during the Great Depression. As Atticus indicates to Jem in Chapter 15, by the time Tom Robinson comes to trial, the Klan is no longer the power it was (although Atticus, a middle-aged man, would certainly remember its activities before the Depression). As Tom's narrow escape from a lynch gang shows, other mobs followed Klan-style patterns of violence, even in the Klan's absence.

Although the Klan was somewhat eclipsed during the time in which *To Kill a Mockingbird* is set, the decade in which Lee wrote her novel is a different matter. After World War II, the third wave of the Klan arose, the 1950s and 1960s seeing a wave of violent Klan activity. 'Klan' in this period no longer refers to a single monolithic organisation: the third wave of the Ku Klux Klan was decentralised, meaning it was made up of a number of separate chapters, such as the White Knights of the Ku Klux Klan (responsible for killing civil rights workers during Freedom Summer in Mississippi in 1964).

Klan violence in the 1950s focused on the Civil Rights Movement. In southern states – particularly Mississippi and Alabama, where much of the worst violence was centred – Klan members forged ties with local government and law enforcement, allowing them to act more openly. The violence in Alabama was such that Birmingham (Alabama's largest city) was nicknamed 'Bombingham'.

Documents compiled by the Southern Poverty Law Center (in Montgomery, Alabama) show that 'the Klan's campaign of terror against the Civil Rights Movement resulted in almost 70 bombings in Georgia and Alabama, the arson of thirty black churches in Mississippi, and 10 racial killings in Alabama alone' (Klanwatch 1997, p.25). Although Klan activities escalated in the early 1960s, in the lead up to desegregation in 1965, the years in which Lee was writing her novel were marked by increasing racial violence in the South, and especially in Alabama.

GENRE, STRUCTURE & LANGUAGE

To Kill a Mockingbird is a cyclical novel, beginning with '[w]hen he was nearly thirteen, my brother Jem got his arm badly broken at the elbow' (p.3) and ending with Jem sedated after this injury. To tell this story, Lee adopts two distinct narrative voices, which some critics call 'Jean Louise' and 'Scout'. The over-arching narrator is the adult Jean Louise, who tells the story retrospectively: 'When enough years had gone by to enable us to look back on them, we sometimes discussed the events leading to his accident. I maintain that the Ewells started it all ...' (p.3). The second narrator is the child Scout: her voice is embedded within Jean Louise's narrative. Because of the child-narrator, *To Kill a Mockingbird* is a *Bildungsroman,* or a coming-of-age narrative (see **Vocabulary**).

Lee shows Scout's coming of age by switching between these narrative voices. When, for example, Aunt Alexandra forces Atticus to explain Finch family history in Chapter 13, Scout tells us, 'I felt myself beginning to cry, but I could not stop,' because she cannot understand her father's curtness (p.147). Jean Louise intrudes to say, 'I know now what he was trying to do, but Atticus was only a man. It takes a woman to do that kind of work' (p.148). Some critics find fault with this narrative technique, with one arguing that Scout has 'the prose style of a well-educated adult' and another that 'Lee's problem has been to tell the story she wants to tell and yet to stay within the consciousness of a child, and she hasn't consistently solved it' (cited in Shields 2007 p.128). The result, however, is that the novel is narrated from the perspective of a child who only appreciates the complexities of the events when she becomes an adult.

The novel also belongs to the category of Southern Literature (see **Vocabulary**). Southern Literature is a conflicted literary category: Lucinda MacKethan (2005) notes that some writers chafe at the fact that criticism of their work is limited by its geographical location. But it remains a useful category for discussing work that is specifically Southern in its language, setting, or themes.

To Kill a Mockingbird is distinctly Southern in its treatment of race and family (see **Themes, Ideas & Values**), but is also saturated in Southern customs and dialect: Part One is particularly rich in such terms. Examples of Southern customs include the emphasis on a deferential form of address for adults: for example, Atticus constantly chides Scout for not calling Boo Radley 'Mr Arthur', and when Mrs Dubose hears Scout and Jem call their father 'Atticus', she calls them the 'sassiest, most disrespectful mutts who ever passed her way' (p.110). Examples of dialect include specifically Southern food and plants, such as Lane cake, scuppernongs, and collards. (See the vocabulary sections of **Chapter-by-Chapter** analysis for a glossary of such terms.) Background events and dialogue show the strong religious sensibilities of the South, as when Jem says that they '[d]on't have any picture shows here, except Jesus ones in the court-house sometimes' (p.8), or Southern pride in their history, as in the pageant where Mrs Merriweather 'chanted mournfully about Maycomb County being older than the state' (p.284).

But the most complicated example of Southern dialect in the novel is the variant terms of address for African-Americans. The dominant term in the novel is 'nigger'. Like 'Negro,' it comes from the Latin word *niger* (meaning 'black') and was originally a neutral term for 'dark-skinned', without offensive intent. By the 1800s, the word had become pejorative, replaced as a general term by 'coloured'. Today, its use is highly offensive in Australia and the United Kingdom and an outright social taboo in the US (barring a recent and specific claiming of the term by African-Americans). The novel's heavy use of this term is a primary reason behind repeated attempts to ban it from schools and libraries.

'Nigger' has two distinct uses in *To Kill a Mockingbird*. When Scout uses the term, she is not consciously seeking to offend. The word is still offensive, perhaps more offensive for the casualness of its use in a child of Scout's background, but Scout uses it as an unthinking reflection of her environment. In correcting her, Atticus hopes to be able to correct the underlying racist patterns of thought that she risks adopting.

When a character such as Bob Ewell uses the word, however, he consciously and deliberately uses it as an insult. Testifying in court, he reaches a crescendo with the explosive claim that '"I seen that black nigger yonder ruttin' on my Mayella!"' (p.190). Ewell is not using 'nigger' unthinkingly or as a neutral term here. By combining it with 'black', he drives home its basis in racial difference, and by using the verb 'rutting', he defines Tom Robinson as an animal rather than as human, an impression he reinforces later by describing the African-American homesteads near his house as 'that nest down yonder' (p.193). This use of 'nigger' typifies the aggression and inherent violence behind the word in the Deep South.

'Nigger' is not the only racially loaded term in the novel. When Mrs Grace Merriweather objects to the dissatisfaction in the African-American community after Tom's conviction, she uses the term 'darky' (p.255). Though 'darky' is also a racially offensive term, Mrs Merriweather either thinks herself more liberal or more refined than Bob Ewell by avoiding 'nigger'. She unthinkingly imitates his animalistic, dehumanising imagery, however, when she says of her African-American housekeeper than an idea 'never entered that wool of hers' (p.257). Varying the terms does not change the underlying ideas.

A less explicitly racist term (especially to readers outside the southern US) is 'boy'. 'Boy' was historically used in British colonies as a term for male (native) servants, but its use is now largely specific to the US. Originally referring to a male slave, it now refers disparagingly to an African-American man. So loaded is the term in this context that the US Supreme Court ruled in 2006 that the term 'boy' alone (rather than, for example, 'black boy') was evidence of discrimination.

More than one character calls Tom Robinson 'boy'. Miss Maudie, for example, calls him '"that boy"' when talking to Jem (p.238), though she shows herself to be of the same liberal mindset as Atticus in referring to Tom's '"coloured friends"' (p.238). Even from this sympathetic character, the term seems infantilising, since Tom is a twenty-five-year-old and married father of three, and clearly no child.

But the strongest example of the discrimination behind 'boy' is in Mr Gilmer's cross-examination of Tom. Mr Gilmer also uses 'nigger', to describe Tom's opponent in an earlier fracas (p.216), and appends 'boy' to the end of almost every question he asks. The effect of this word – benign in other contexts – is such that Dill 'started crying and couldn't stop' (p.219). He explains to Scout that '"[t]he way that man called him 'boy' all the time and sneered at him' had made him '"sick, plain sick"' (p.219).

Through Scout's unthinking mimicry, Atticus' teaching, Bob Ewell's aggression and Dill's sensitivity, Lee outlines the complexity of racial invective in the dialects of the Deep South.

CHAPTER-BY-CHAPTER ANALYSIS

Part One

Chapters 1–3

Summary: *Introduction to Maycomb and to the main characters; Scout begins school.*

Chapter 1 introduces Maycomb:

- Scout describes Maycomb as 'an old town, but it was a tired old town when I first knew it' (p.5).

- The description of Maycomb in this chapter indicates that it is slow moving and insular: Scout notes that 'There was no hurry, for there was nowhere to go, nothing to buy and no money to buy it with, nothing to see outside the boundaries of Maycomb County' (p.6).

- This chapter establishes the background for Tom Robinson's trial: the trial will attract a picnic atmosphere because there's nothing to do in Maycomb, but the outcome is inevitable because Maycomb is culturally conservative.

This first chapter also hints at events that are not significant until the final chapters, such as Jem's broken arm. But although the chapter begins with Scout's reflection that she and Jem 'sometimes discussed the events leading to his accident' (p.3), Tom's trial is only hinted at as a traumatic event that Scout says they can't bring themselves to discuss until 'enough years had gone by to enable us to look back' (p.3).

Chapters 2 and 3 show Scout's first day at school, which she finds restrictive. The school episodes serve two main purposes. First, school separates Scout from her peers.

- School foregrounds Atticus' unusual parenting: he has authority but treats his children as peers, assuming them capable of adult, rational debate. Miss Caroline, in contrast, treats her students as children even though many work as adults. As a result, her authority is negligible.

- These chapters also establish Scout as a plausible child-narrator, revealing her intelligence and her exposure to complex ideas.

Secondly, school introduces the readers to characters who become important later in the novel: the Cunninghams, who reappear at significant moments, and the Ewells, the catalyst for the trial.

KEY POINTS

Lee references numerous popular novels in this early section: *The Gray Ghost: The Return of Stoner's Boy*; the *Rover Boys* novels; the Tom Swift novels and Edgar Rice Burroughs' novels about Tarzan and John Carter, hero of Mars. These young boys' novels enrich Scout's experience of growing up in the Deep South in the 1930s and reinforce her status as a tomboy. They also underscore the children's melodramatic attitude towards Boo Radley (whom they see as a creature of legend, not a person) and their reactions to the traumas of the trial: in books such as these, villains are clearly demarcated and endings are happy.

Key Vocabulary

Andrew Jackson: seventh president of the United States; campaigned in Georgia against Seminole and Creek Indians during the First Seminole War (1817–18).

Code of Alabama: compilation of the state's laws on criminal offences. Its 'unsullied' nature reflects Atticus' distaste for criminal law.

Collard: leafy green vegetable grown in the southern United States; a distinctly Southern food.

Dewey Decimal system: Melvil Dewey's system for library classification, developed in 1876. Despite Jem's statement, it is not an education method. (He may be confusing it with the experiential educational philosophy of John Dewey, popular in the 1930s.) The reference here suggests that people are 'classified' in Maycomb.

Entailment: a legal limitation requiring land to pass to a specified sequence of heirs and not be sold, divided, or bequeathed elsewhere.

Flivver: slang for a car, especially an old one (sometimes specifically the Model-T Ford).

Haint: Southern dialect term for 'ghost'.

Hoover carts: Great Depression-era carts made by cutting the front section of a car away and drawing the rear section behind a horse. Named (sarcastically) after then-President Herbert Hoover.

John Wesley: Anglican cleric and founder of the Methodist movement.

Lorenzo Dow: itinerant American preacher, broadly Methodist in approach.

Methodists: the persecution of Methodists is separate from the white colonisation of the US by persecuted Puritans, who fled Europe in the early 1600s. The Methodists fled England in the mid-1700s.

Stumphole whisky: homemade whisky (see 'shinny' in Chapter 13).

WPA: Works Progress Administration, created in 1935 by President Roosevelt to create jobs during the Great Depression, usually building work on public buildings or roads. The reference is anachronistic here, since this section takes place in 1933.

Q What is the significance of Scout saying, 'Until I feared I would lose it, I never loved to read. One does not love breathing' (p.20)?

Chapters 4–8

Summary: *Scout, Jem, and Dill continue their obsession with Boo Radley, which comes to Mr Nathan Radley's attention.*

In these chapters, the children become increasingly obsessed with Boo Radley. Boo is no longer a neighbourhood myth, as he was in the early chapters. His relationship with the children becomes interactive:

- Jem and Scout find small treasures hidden in the Radley oaks. The treasures are easily hoarded items: some are only treasures to their original owner (the spelling medal) and some show Boo becoming as interested in the children as they are in him (the soap carvings).

- Jem, far more emotionally involved with Boo than Scout is, seeks to interact in return, by passing a letter to Boo '"askin' him real politely to come out sometimes, and tell us what he does in there"' (p.52) and later trying to peer through the windows of the house.

- They approach the Radley house more frequently: Jem, reluctant to touch the house in Chapter 1 (p.16), voluntarily approaches it four times in these chapters.

- They construct a melodrama around Boo's life, enacting it daily until Atticus insists that they stop '"putting his life's history on display for the edification of the neighbourhood"' (p.55). Atticus believes the children are mocking Boo, but the children's protestations suggest they're trying to comprehend a bewildering situation.

- Jem comes to see Boo as benevolent: though frightened when Boo mends his trousers, he cries when Mr Nathan blocks up the knothole.

- Scout, younger than Jem, still thinks Boo is malevolent: his laughter when she hits the house after rolling in the tire frightens her, and she says she 'nearly threw up' (p.80) when she realises he has put the blanket around her during the fire. Not until Scout is nine (Jem's age at the beginning of the novel) does she see Boo as sympathetic (see p.267, for example).

Key Vocabulary

Brigadier General Joe Wheeler: Confederate cavalry general in the US Civil War.

Hoodoo: African-American traditional folk magic, also called 'conjure'. Distinct from Haitian or Louisiana Voodoo, which is a religion.

Indian head penny: one-cent coin minted between 1859 and 1909, sometimes used as protective talismans in hoodoo.

Little Three Eyes: character from a Brothers Grimm fairy tale, who failed to fall asleep when enchanted because of her third eye.

Morphodite: colloquial pronunciation of 'hermaphrodite', a person with the reproductive organs of both sexes. 'Morphodite' also indicates that the snowman's mixture of snow and dirt makes it both white and black.

Rosetta Stone: Egyptian artefact that enabled modern understanding of hieroglyphics.

Scuppernongs: muscadine grape variety native to the south-eastern United States.

Second Battle of the Marne: last major German offensive on the Western Front in World War I.

Squaw: Native American woman (offensive).

Q Why does Nathan Radley block the hole in the oak? What effect does this have on the narrative?

Chapters 9–11

Summary: *The Finches celebrate Christmas at Finch's Landing, and Atticus gives two lessons in courage.*

These chapters introduce members of the extended Finch family: Uncle Jack, Aunt Alexandra, and cousin Francis Hancock. The visit to Finch's Landing reveals Finch family history, enriching our understanding of their social position and of later events:

- Their plantation background lingers in the 'two-storeyed white house with porches circling it upstairs and downstairs' (p.88).

- Their slave-owning past is evident in the 'traces of an old cotton landing' and Scout's reference to the 'Finch Negroes' (p.88).

- The restricted lives of Southern women are shown in the peculiar Daughters' Staircase, which forced Finch women to enter their bedroom through their parents' bedroom, and in Aunt Alexandra's frustration when Scout resists the feminine practices of 'playing with small stoves, tea sets, and wearing the Add-A-Pearl necklace she gave [her] when [she] was born' (p.90).

The Finches' past as southern plantation owners, dependent on the slave economy, lingers in Francis, who prompts Scout to break her no-fighting rule by calling Atticus a 'nigger-lover' (p.92).

Jack's presence allows Atticus to discuss Tom's case with another adult:

- When talking to an adult, Atticus is pessimistic, telling Jack that it '"couldn't be worse"' (p.97) and insisting, '"[y]ou know what's going to happen as well as I do"' (p.98).

- Atticus also confesses to Jack that he'd '"hoped to get through life without a case of this kind' (p.98), revealing that he's not defending Tom by choice.

- Like Scout – who says that it 'was not until many years later that I realized he wanted me to hear every word he said' (p.98) – the reader doesn't appreciate the full impact of this discussion until after Tom's inevitable conviction.

KEY POINTS

Chapter 10 introduces and explains the novel's primary metaphor when Atticus says to Jem, '"Shoot all the bluejays you want, if you can hit 'em, but remember it's a sin to kill a mockingbird"' (p.99). Miss Maudie elaborates: '"Mockingbirds don't do one thing but make music for us to enjoy. They don't eat up people's gardens, don't nest in corncribs, they don't do one thing but sing their hearts out for us. That's why it's a sin to kill a mockingbird"' (pp.99– 100). In chapter 25, after Tom's death, BB Underwood writes a stinging editorial arguing that 'it was a sin to kill cripples, be they standing, sitting, or escaping' (p.265). The similarity of these two phrases positions Tom as the first of the titular mockingbirds. As Jem and Scout walk past the Radley house on their way to the pageant, 'a solitary mocker poured out his repertoire in blissful unawareness of whose tree he sat in' (p.281). This return to the mockingbird metaphor prefigures Scout's description of Boo as a mockingbird in Chapter 30, when she says that to expose him to a trial for murdering Bob Ewell would '"be sort of like shootin' a mockingbird, wouldn't it?"' (p.304). Boo Radley is also the mockingbird of the title.

Key Vocabulary

Camellia: state flower of Alabama.

Corncrib: ventilated structure for the storage of unhusked corn, where it can be dried for later use.

Dixie Howell: Alabama college football player from 1932 to 1934.

Druthers: a person's own way, choice, or preference.

General Hood: Confederate general in the Civil War.

Jew's harp: simple musical instrument made of a lyre-shaped metal frame and a metal tongue, played by plucking the tongue.

John Hale: Uncle Jack's name recalls John Hale, minister from Beverley, who first presided over and then denounced the Salem Witch Trials in 1692, made famous by Arthur Miller's play *The Crucible* (1952).

Lafayette: Mrs Dubose is named for Gilbert du Motier, Marquis de Lafayette, a French aristocrat who served as a general in the American War of Independence.

Lord Melbourne: Queen Victoria's first Prime Minister and mentor.

Rose Aylmer: sister of the 5th Baron Aylmer, and subject of a romantic poem by Walter Savage Landor.

Stonewall Jackson: Confederate general in the Civil War.

Waiting on tenterhooks: in a state of painful suspense or uneasy anxiety.

Q Does Atticus' ambivalence about taking Tom's case affect the courage of his stand?

Part Two

Chapters 12–14

Summary: *Calpurnia's church, Aunt Alexandra's arrival, and lessons in breeding.*

In narrative terms, First Purchase African ME Church does for Maycomb's African-American community what Finch's Landing did in Chapter 9: it gives a sense of a conflicted past:

- The church is 'outside the southern town limits, across the old sawmill tracks' (p.130). The building's isolation – outside both white homes and white industry – reflects Jim Crow segregation.

- First Purchase is so named because it was 'paid for from the first earnings of freed slaves' (p.130).
First Purchase also represents a conflicted present:

- When Jem and Scout appear, 'the men stepped back and took off their hats; the women crossed their arms at the waist, weekday gestures of respectful attention' (p.131). The children's appearance brings segregation to this African-American church.

- Although built from the earnings of freed slaves, the church is not an exclusively African-American place: 'Negroes worshipped in it on Sundays and white men gambled in it on weekdays' (p.130). Reverend Sykes's sermon warns his flock against 'the evils of heady brews, gambling, and strange women' (p.134), but the white community co-opts the church for activities that the church itself denounces.

- The church shows signs of a specifically African-American culture, as where 'Lightening [sic] rods guarding some graves denoted dead who rested uneasily' (p.130). This is analogous to the hoodoo that Scout fears (p.66) or the Hot Steams that allegedly haunt the roads (p.41). These cultural markers are openly displayed here, where elsewhere the dominant white culture dismisses them as 'nigger-talk' (p.41).

This single instance of insider engagement with Maycomb's African-American community reveals the environment in which Tom Robinson lives and works. Just as Chapter 12 shows African-American life, Chapter 13 is devoted to Aunt Alexandra's teachings on the history and culture of Maycomb's white community (see **Themes, Ideas & Values**). The sharp opposition between the dominant white culture and the repressed African-American culture in these chapters highlights Atticus' more liberal outlook.

KEY POINT

Calpurnia tells Jem and Scout that she taught her son Zeebo to read from Blackstone's Commentaries. *Commentaries on the Laws of England*, by Sir William Blackstone, was published between 1765 and 1769 and is the source of a principle in criminal law known as 'Blackstone's formulation' (sometimes called 'Blackstone's ratio' or 'the Blackstone ratio'): 'better that ten guilty persons escape than that one innocent suffer'. The principle is closely tied to the presumption of innocence in criminal law. Without specifically mentioning Blackstone's formulation here, Lee probably expects at least some of her readers to be familiar with it. This adds weight to the fact that Tom Robinson does not receive a fair trial, since he is presumed guilty rather than innocent.

Key Vocabulary

Asafoetida: soft, brown gum resin with a bitter, acrid taste. Used in India and the Middle East as a spice. Also used in perfumes, which is probably the case here.

Lane cake: traditional Southern cake for special occasions. The recipe was first published in Alabama in 1898.

Rice Christian: pejorative term for someone declaring themselves a Christian for material rather than religious reasons.

Shadrach: biblical figure, otherwise known as Hananiah. One of three young Jewish men brought to the court of Nebuchadnezzar II, king of Babylon. Thrown into a fiery furnace for refusing to bow to Nebuchadnezzar's statue, they were preserved by their faith.

Shinny: shortened form of 'moonshine', or illegal alcohol, a usage apparently specific to *To Kill a Mockingbird*. Drinking is still frowned on in Maycomb two years after the repeal of Prohibition (the national banning of the production, sale, or consumption of alcohol).

Snuff: a tobacco preparation, which can either be powdered and inhaled or placed between the gum and cheek.

Tight: slang term meaning drunk or tipsy.

Q What role do African-American superstitions play in the novel?

Chapters 15–16

Summary: The attempted lynching and the beginning of Tom's trial.

These chapters centre on two different gangs of men. The first gang, headed by Heck Tate, warns Atticus of threats to lynch Tom before his trial.

- Scout says, 'In Maycomb, grown men stood outside in the front yard for only two reasons: death and politics' (p.159). Scout assumes the group is reporting a death, but Jem is aware that they could equally be threatening a death.

- To the listeners in the house, the group seems threatening, such as when Link Deas says, '"You've got everything to lose from this, Atticus"' (p.160) and when '[t]here was a murmur among the group of men, made more ominous when Atticus moved back to the bottom front step and the men drew nearer to him' (p.161).

- When Jem disrupts the group, the children notice that 'they were people we saw every day' (p.161). Although Atticus says 'those were our friends' (p.161), Jem refuses to acknowledge that this means they wouldn't hurt Atticus.

- Here, Jem seems more realistic than Atticus, who claims that the Klan '"was a political organization more than anything else"' (p.161) and that '"It'll never come back"' (p.162). In 1960, readers knew that the Klan had already come back and that, moreover, in Alabama it had close ties to law enforcement. Atticus himself would remember that the gang that lynched Leo Frank in 1915 included a minister, two former appellate court judges and a former sheriff.

The second gang comes to lynch Tom the night before his trial. While the threatening nature of the previous night's gang might have been illusory, this gang intends to murder Tom.

- Lynching was not only a form of extra-judicial execution, but also an act of terror. The body was displayed publicly, as a warning to other African-Americans who might step out of line. Lynching often had some measure of support from the community: earlier, Cecil Jacobs taunted Scout in the schoolyard, saying, '"[m]y folks said your daddy was a disgrace, an' that nigger oughta hang from the water-tank"' (p.85).

- The gang note that they've drawn off Heck Tate and his men by sending them on a 'snipe hunt' (p.167) (see below). Since Tate, an experienced law-enforcement officer, knows about the lynching threats, his absence is perhaps suspicious.

The trial itself is marked by a picnic atmosphere:

- The event literally becomes a picnic, with families eating on the lawn outside the courthouse.

- It draws people from across the social spectrum, including '[p]eople from the south end of the county' and the Mennonites 'who lived deep in the woods, did most of their trading across the river, and rarely came to Maycomb' (p.174).

- Miss Maudie is the only absent person; she declares it 'morbid' (p.175) and says, '"Just because it's public, I don't have to go"' (p.176).

Key Vocabulary

Braxton Bragg: Confederate general of the Civil War.

Mennonites: general term for numerous Christian Anabaptist denominations. These seem to be conservative Mennonites: like the Amish, they favour social separation, plain clothing, and simple living.

Nehi Cola: flavoured soft drinks, originally marketed in Georgia.

Picnic: a persistent interpretation (largely propagated online) suggests that 'picnic' is a racist term related to lynching, but this is a false etymology.

Snipe hunt: also called a fool's errand, a type of wild-goose chase that sets inexperienced people an impossible or even imaginary task.

Q What is the narrative significance of these two gangs appearing back-to-back in the novel?

Chapters 17–21

Summary: *Tom's trial and conviction.*

As Atticus says to Jack in Chapter 9, '"[t]he evidence boils down to you did, I didn't"' (p.97).

- Since no doctor was called (p.184), there's no evidence of the rape apart from the Ewells' statements.

- Atticus doesn't seem to have heard full witness statements prior to the trial. Tate reacts 'as if something had suddenly been made plain to him' when testifying about Mayella's bruises (p.185). Atticus reacts the same way: '[s]omething had been made plain to Atticus, also, and it brought him to his feet' (p.185). This suggests that Atticus has not previously considered the injuries as evidence of Tom's innocence.

In these chapters, two significant characters speak for themselves for the only time in the novel:

- Mayella Ewell, whose accusation prompts this trial, is not mentioned prior to it. The only reference after the trial is when Atticus says of Bob, '"if spitting in my face and threatening me saved Mayella Ewell one extra beating, that's something I'll gladly take"' (p.241).

- Tom Robinson speaks directly here for the only time in the novel, apart from two sentences to Atticus after the attempted lynching. All his later appearances are reported by other characters: he never speaks for himself again.

Tom's testimony is loaded speech, subject to interpretation and manipulation:

- Scout interprets Tom's comment that '"I didn't wanta be ugly, I didn't wanta push her or nothing"' to mean that his 'manners were as good as Atticus" (p.215). Later, Atticus explains that this seeming politeness is fear: 'he would not have dared strike a white woman under any circumstances and expect to live long' (p.215).

- When Mr Gilmer cross-examines Tom, he concentrates less on facts than on manipulating Tom's perceived attitude. For example, when Tom reports being '"scared I'd hafta face up to what I didn't do"', Mr Gilmer responds, '"Are you being impudent to me, boy?"' (p.219). Tom's guilt becomes a question of whether he is stepping out of his social sphere, not a question of the practicalities of the crime.

- The most significant example is when Tom explains why he performed Mayella's chores without pay: '"I felt right sorry for her, she seemed to try more'n the rest of 'em"' (p.217). Gilmer reacts with horror: '"*You* felt sorry for *her*, you felt *sorry* for her?"' (p.218).

Through Tom's testimony, the reader sees behaviours normally considered positive, such as compassion and kindness, treated as criminal.

Atticus' summing up foregrounds the argument that, in his words, '"[t]his case is as simple as black and white"' (p.224):

- He foregrounds Tom's race, describing Mayella's testimony as '"a lie as black as Tom Robinson's skin"' (p.225), an unfortunate simile under the circumstances.

- He condemns the racist stereotype '"that *all* Negroes lie, that *all* Negroes are basically immoral beings, that *all* Negro men are not to be trusted with our women"' (p.225). If he can't shake the jury's belief in this stereotype, they might still accept his implicit argument that Tom – '"a quiet, respectable, humble Negro"' (p.225) – is the exception to this rule.

Key Vocabulary:

Cotton gin: a machine (comprising a cylinder, wire teeth, and a wire screen) that separates cotton fibres from the seeds, a process originally done by hand. It revolutionised the South's economy and reignited pro-slavery arguments (since more slaves were needed to pick the vast amounts of cotton that could now be separated daily).

Ex cathedra: (literally 'from the chair') used originally for pronouncements from the pope that were considered infallible.

Q Does Atticus actually have a good defence for Tom Robinson?

Chapters 22–25

Summary: *Maycomb's reaction to the trial; Bob Ewell's threats; Tom's death.*

The town settles down after Tom's trial. Jem is devastated and Atticus bitter (though he denies it), but the general population is neither surprised nor alarmed by the verdict: in Miss Rachel's words, 'if a man like Atticus Finch wants to butt his head against a stone wall, it's his head' (p.236).

These chapters set up the events for the end of the novel, particularly Bob Ewell's revenge:

- Atticus asks Jem to '"see if you can stand in Bob Ewell's shoes a minute"' (p.241), mimicking his earlier dictum that you can't understand a person '"until you climb into his skin and walk around in it"' (p.33).

- Atticus, however, fails to climb into Bob's skin. Insistent that Bob '"got it all out of his system that morning"' (p.241), he does not anticipate coming events.

- Jem decides society includes four types of people, each of whom looks down on the group below: '"our kind of folks don't like the

Cunninghams, the Cunninghams don't like the Ewells, and the Ewells hate and despise the coloured folks"' (p.249).

- Scout disagrees: '"I think there's just one kind of folks. Folks"' (p.250). This conversation and Scout's plans to socialise with Walter Cunningham Jr, show her maturation from the thoughtless child at the novel's beginning, who mocked Walter's table manners and protested, '"He ain't company, Cal, he's just a Cunningham"' (p.27).

Tom's death is juxtaposed with the Maycomb missionary tea, at which Mrs Grace Merriweather describes 'the squalid lives of the Mrunas' (p.251):

- Mrs Merriweather's hypocrisy is evident in her secret alcoholism, one of Maycomb's open secrets. Scout muses earlier that 'if Mrs Grace Merriweather sips gin out of Lydia E. Pinkham bottles it's nothing unusual – her mother did the same' (p.145).

- Mrs Merriweather tells Scout that she's lucky to '"live in a Christian home with Christian folks in a Christian land"' (p.255). Christianity is Mrs Merriweather's solution to all problems: she suggests, for example, that First Purchase should approach Helen Robinson to '"help her lead a Christian life for those children from here on out"' (p.255).

- Mrs Merriweather and the missionary society see Christianity as something to be imposed on the African-American community: says Mrs Farrow, '"We can educate 'em till we're blue in the face, we can try till we drop to make Christians out of 'em ..."' (p.256).

Atticus' announcement of Tom's death follows immediately after Mrs Merriweather's endorsement of segregation.

Key Point

Tom's running is a repeated motif throughout this section of the book: he runs rather than physically repulse Mayella; he runs when Bob Ewell attacks Mayella; and he runs rather than wait for Atticus' appeal. Running is the only defence left to Tom, but running is, in Atticus' words, 'a sure sign of guilt' (p.215). In the case of the escape attempt, Tom's defensive behaviour is punished by execution. The town's attitude is summed up after his death: 'To Maycomb, Tom's death was typical. Typical of a nigger to cut and run. Typical of a nigger's mentality to have no plan, no thought for the future, just run blind first chance he saw' (p.265).

Q Does the novel support Jem's idea that background is '"how long your family's been readin' and writin"' (p.250)?

Chapters 26–28

Summary: *Scout's return to school; the Halloween pageant.*

Returning to school reignites Scout's interest in Boo Radley:

- Scout feels remorse 'at ever having taken part in what must have been sheer torment to Arthur Radley' (p.267) but Atticus, not discerning her change in attitude, forbids her to harass Boo.

- Scout's new fantasy centres on Boo becoming part of her daily life. This foreshadows her later awareness that Boo is too damaged ever to be comfortable in conventional society.

Scout and Jem remain anxious after the summer's events, which 'hung over us like smoke in a closed room' (p.268):

- Scout remembers walking past Mrs Dubose every day, something that, like the now-unspoken events of the trial, was endured rather than confronted.

- Scout struggles with the discrepancy between the wholesale condemnation of Hitler at school and Tom's conviction: her teacher claims in the classroom that '"[o]ver here we don't believe in persecuting anybody. Persecution comes from people who are prejudiced"' (p.270), while at the trial Scout overheard her saying that 'it's time somebody taught 'em a lesson, they were gettin' way above themselves' (p.272). Scout can't reconcile the hypocrisy, but Cecil Jacobs can: reflecting on the long persecution of Jewish people, he says, '"that ain't no cause to persecute 'em. They're white, ain't they?"' (p.271).

Bob Ewell steps up his persecution of the people involved in the trial:

- He approaches Judge Taylor's house, assuming it to be empty.

- His harassment of Helen Robinson is more sustained, until he's confronted by Link Deas.

- Both acts show that Bob will not confront anyone as strong as himself.

Bob Ewell's attack on the children is one of the novel's more intense passages:

- Because Scout, out of embarrassment, has refused to take off her ham costume, she can't see the attack. Scout describes it entirely in terms of her other senses: she 'felt the sand go cold under [her] feet' (p.288), 'felt Jem's hand leave [her]' (p.289) and heard Boo 'groan and pull something heavy along the ground' (p.289).

- Because Scout is a first-person narrator, the reader also can't see the attack. Not being able to see increases the anxiety of the attack for both Scout and the reader.

- The readers' inability to 'see' the attack also increases the tension of the coming chapters, since they, like Atticus, have to be convinced of Jem's innocence.

Key Vocabulary

Ad Astra Per Aspera: literally, 'to the stars through difficulties'.

Bob Taylor: Federal judge from Tennessee.

Cotton Tom Heflin: US senator for Alabama and leading proponent of white supremacy.

Ladies Law: Alabama's criminal code forbade the use of abusive, insulting, or obscene language in front of women. (This was also one of the charges against the young Boo Radley.)

National Recovery Act: enacted in 1933, authorising the US President to regulate industry, in an attempt to stimulate the Depression-era economy. Widely considered a failure even at the time.

Yankee: used outside the US to describe any American. In the US south, it refers to an inhabitant of the north-eastern states, which fought against the Confederacy in the Civil War.

Q Does the novel support Atticus' claim that 'after enough time passed people would forget that Tom Robinson's existence was ever brought to their attention' (p.268)?

Chapters 29–31

Summary: Scout relates the attack; Scout meets Boo Radley; Atticus and Heck Tate agree to cover up Boo's crime.

Heck Tate finds Bob '"with a kitchen knife stuck up under his ribs"' (p.294). The knife is the only real evidence against Boo:

- Bob Ewell, intending murder, provides himself with the more conventional switchblade.

- Boo uses the only kind of weapon available to him, an ordinary household implement.

- The kitchen knife also suggests that the attack could be seen as pre-meditated murder, since Boo went armed with a deadly weapon.

- By removing Bob's switchblade, Heck Tate implies that Bob was killed with his own weapon. If he went to trial, Boo would then be tried for either self-defence or manslaughter, both less serious offences (in a legal sense) than pre-meditated murder.

Bob Ewell's attack shows a flaw in Atticus' favoured policy of walking in another man's shoes before judging him:

- Atticus cannot comprehend Bob's mindset. He cannot even articulate it: '"I can't conceive of a man who'd —"' (p.296). While Atticus thought Bob was merely posturing, both Jem and Aunt Alexandra knew Bob was a threat.

- Heck Tate is unconcerned about Bob's motivations: '"there's just some kind of men you have to shoot before you can say hidy to 'em. Even then, they ain't worth the bullet it takes to shoot 'em"' (p.296).

- Tate suggests that Bob's death is justice, not murder: '"There's a black boy dead for no reason, and the man responsible for it's dead. Let the dead bury the dead this time, Mr Finch"' (p.304). This attitude raises uncomfortable questions about other extra-judicial actions, such as the planned lynching and Tom's death.

Atticus has been the moral centre of the novel to this point. But whichever reading of the attack he accepts, he faces a moral dilemma:

- If he believes Jem killed Bob, his twelve-year-old son must face a trial that will be traumatic even if it is '"clear-cut self-defence"' (p.300). Atticus knows the trial will be traumatic, and sounds more bitter than at any other point in the novel when he says, '"[l]et the county come and bring sandwiches"' (p.301).

- If he accepts that Boo killed Bob, involving the law would force a reclusive, damaged man through a terrible ordeal. In Tate's words, '"taking the one man who's done you and this town a great service an' draggin' him with his shy ways into the limelight – to me, that's a sin"' (p.304).

- Scout fulfils her neighbourly fantasy of interacting with Boo:

- She slots Boo into her idea of how neighbours behave: 'Neighbours bring food with death and flowers with sickness and little things in between' (p.307).

- She also recognises that she and Jem have not behaved as neighbours should: '[b]ut neighbours give in return. We had never put back into the tree what we took out of it: we had given him nothing' (p.307).

The novel ends by restoring equilibrium: Scout runs over the novel's events but ends with Atticus' constant presence, suggesting a return to calm.

Q Is it true that Scout and Jem have given Boo nothing?

CHARACTERS & RELATIONSHIPS

Atticus Finch

Key Quotes

'"Atticus Finch is the same in his house as he is on the public streets."' (p.51)

'"Whether Maycomb knows it or not, we're paying him the highest tribute we can pay a man. We trust him to do right. It's that simple."' (p.261)

Though Scout is the narrator, Atticus is perhaps the central character. His decision to defend Tom Robinson – not simply to act as his court-appointed lawyer but to offer the best possible defence – is the catalyst for the events of the novel. He is also the novel's moral centre, since Scout and Jem are still developing their own moral codes and are learning them, in part, from their father. As he says to Heck Tate at the end of the novel, '"if they don't trust me they won't trust anybody"' (p.301).

Atticus is the elder son of a formerly wealthy plantation (and slave-owning) family, who is 'related by blood or marriage to nearly every family in the town' (p.5). He has defied family tradition by leaving the family homestead to study law in Montgomery. Scout mentions that Atticus has had a 'profound distaste for the practice of criminal law' (p.5) since his first clients were hanged. In the novel, we see him concentrating on other aspects of the law, such as Walter Cunningham's entailment, until Tom's trial.

The events before Tom's trial show different facets of Atticus' character: he admires courage, believes his skill with a gun is an unfair advantage and desires to treat damaged characters, such as Boo Radley, with respect. But his essential character remains unchanged for much of the novel. He is the same man during and after Tom's trial as he was before it: courteous, well-read, drily humourous, an attentive father, a fond brother, and, above all, a man who believes that '"[y]ou never really understand a person until you consider things from his point of view"' (p.33).

Atticus' great moral dilemma is not whether or not to defend Tom Robinson: once he has made that decision, he never wavers, even though he'd '"hoped to get through life without a case of this kind"' (p.98). Atticus' moral dilemma lies in the death of Bob Ewell. When he believes Jem has killed Bob, he doesn't hesitate to say that Jem must be prosecuted. When he realises that Boo is the killer, he does hesitate. This shifts the novel's central image of Atticus, Miss Maudie's idea that 'Atticus Finch is the same in his house as he is on the public streets'. Scout, during Tom's trial, repeats this with a significant twist: '"He's the same in the court-room as he is on the public streets"' (p.220). Atticus' decision to accept Tate's idea of justice, rather than the law, shows him compromising for the first time.

Scout (Jean Louise) Finch

KEY QUOTES

'"Scout'd just as soon jump on someone as look at him if her pride's at stake ..."' (p.97)

'I suggested that one could be a ray of sunshine in pants just as well [as in a dress], but Aunty said that one had to behave like a sunbeam, that I was born good but had grown progressively worse every year.' (p.90)

The reader sees the novel's events through Scout's eyes. As a child, she is hot-tempered and aggressive, automatically responding with her fists to any perceived insult or slight. She speaks her mind without thinking, as when she criticises Walter Cunningham's table manners (pp.26–7). She's impatient of restraint, including resisting her aunt's attempts to mould her into a Southern belle, a fate that she describes as 'the starched walls of a pink cotton penitentiary' (p.150).

Despite this, Scout is confident in her own environment. At school, for example, the students choose Scout to explain to Miss Caroline the intricacies of county society (p.22). However, Scout, while clever, is also uncritical: it takes Atticus' careful teaching (supported by Calpurnia, Aunt Alexandra, and Miss Maudie) to point out how she unthinkingly reflects her environment and to show her that concepts such as race are more complicated than they seem.

Atticus is more worried by Scout than by Jem (p.97) and is desperate to see her through the ordeal of Tom's trial '"without bitterness, and most of all, without catching Maycomb's usual disease"' (p.98). Part of this process involves gradually changing her attitude. When he tells her not to say 'nigger' because it's 'common' (p.83), for example, he's guiding her away from both her own childish characteristics and the prejudices of her community: Scout complains that it's '"what everybody at school says"', but Atticus simply responds, '"[f]rom now on it'll be everybody less one"' (p.83). He wishes her to be aware of her community without uncritically accepting all its flaws and prejudices.

Scout's rough edges are smoothed away during the novel: she stops swearing (except under extreme provocation) and she is never as violent after Atticus extracts a promise that she will not fight on his behalf (p.84). But she is still so young at the end of the novel that most of her development occurs later. The reader doesn't see these changes, but deduces them from the adult Jean Louise's narration. Jean Louise is reflective rather than hot-tempered and thoughtless, newly sympathetic to Aunt Alexandra's perspective and able to see more than one side of an issue.

Jem Finch

Key Quotes

'Jem, educated on a half-Decimal half-Dunce-cap basis, seemed to function effectively alone or in a group ...' (p.36)

'Jem was not one to dwell on past defeats ...' (p.57)

Four years older than Scout, Jem is her confidante and primary playmate. During the first part of the novel, he is as much a child as Scout: he's superstitious and prone to swift retribution. But the novel's second part opens with 'Jem was twelve. He was difficult to live with, inconsistent, moody' (p.127). He is treated as an adult: Calpurnia calls him 'Mister Jem' (p.127) and Miss Maudie stops baking child-size cakes for him (p.237).

Jem's maturity allows him to understand the abstract issues at stake in Tom's trial better than Scout. His sensitivity to such things is foreshadowed in his silent tears when Nathan Radley blocks up the hollow oak (p.70) and in the episode with the rabid dog, when he tells Scout that Atticus' refusal to boast about his shooting skill is '"something you wouldn't understand"' (p.109). Later, the reader sees that Jem is terrified when Scout leaps into the lynch mob (p.167), and how 'his shoulders jerked as if each "guilty" was a separate stab between them' (p.233) when Tom's verdict is read out.

Jem may be old enough to understand the abstract issues of the trial, but he is young enough (or sensitive enough) to be deeply hurt by injustice. Atticus suggests this is a question of maturity, not personality: after the attempted lynching, he tells Jem, '"you'll understand folks a little better when you're older"' (p.173), and after the verdict suggests, '"[s]o far nothing in your life has interfered with your reasoning process"' (p.243). But Jem perhaps has a perceptivity that Atticus lacks: for example, Jem's fears of Bob Ewell's revenge turn out to be more accurate than Atticus' optimism.

Jem's maturation foreshadows Scout's. Scout muses, 'I hoped Jem would understand folks a little better when he was older; I wouldn't' (p.173). But by the novel's end, Scout – about the same age as Jem was in the first chapter, and just beginning to understand the 'sheer torment' (p.267) that they must have caused Boo Radley – takes the same first step towards maturity as Jem.

Boo (Arthur) Radley

Key Quotes

'Boo was about six-and-a-half feet tall, judging from his tracks; he dined on raw squirrels and any cats he could catch, that's why his hands were blood-stained ...' (p.14)

'[H]e's crazy, I reckon, like they say, but Atticus, I swear to God he ain't ever harmed us, he ain't ever hurt us, he coulda cut my throat from ear to ear that night but he tried to mend my pants instead ...' (p.80)

Boo Radley is the novel's clearest example of a Southern Gothic character: a mildly rebellious boy who transgresses against the South's moral code, is imprisoned by his family and slowly fades into a ghostly recluse. The most significant changes to Boo have already occurred before the novel begins, morphing him from a boy who '"[s]poke as nicely as he knew how"' (p.51) to a terrified recluse who is shaken by 'a strange small spasm ... as if he heard fingernails scrape slate' (p.298) when he meets someone's eyes. The psychological shift is accompanied by physical changes. Although Boo doesn't match Jem's far-fetched image of him, Scout tells us he has 'sickly white hands that had never seen the sun' and 'grey eyes so colourless [she] thought he was blind' (p.298). His disconnection extends to his immediate surroundings: Scout notes that '[e]very move he made was uncertain, as if he were not sure his hands and feet could make proper contact with the things he touched' (p.305).

For the reader (and Scout), Boo seems to change radically across the novel, but much of this is illusory, arising from Scout's better knowledge of him. Scout and Jem are the only children in a settled neighbourhood, so they represent a new experience for Boo. Presumably, their youth is what appeals to him, because his own life was truncated when he became involved with the Cunningham gang from Old Sarum in his teens. The treasures he leaves them are children's treasures: lucky pennies, carved dolls, spelling medals, chewing gum. Despite the one-way nature of their relationship, Boo feels strongly enough about them to leave the house when they're attacked.

Boo's emergence is only temporary. After he re-enters the Radley house, Scout says, 'I never saw him again' (p.306). Though the initial damage was done by his family's excessive punishment of youthful misdemeanours, Boo is now his own jailer. As Miss Maudie says, '"Arthur Radley just stays in the house, that's all … Wouldn't you stay in the house if you didn't want to come out?"' (p.49).

Key Point

The novel contains two other characters whose significance to the plot is disproportionate to their actual appearance in the text. Tom Robinson and Mayella Ewell are central to the rape trial. Mayella, in particular, is the novel's catalyst: without her accusation, there is no plot. But both characters are otherwise marginalised by or even absent from the novel. One question to consider here is whether these two characters speak freely to the reader and whether we hear their full stories.

Tom Robinson

Key Quotes

'If he had been whole, he would have been a fine specimen of a man.' (p.212)

'"What was one Negro, more or less, among two hundred of 'em? He wasn't Tom to them, he was an escaping prisoner."' (p.260)

The reader gathers a reasonable amount of biographical information about Tom: he's twenty-five and married, with three children (p.210); he's been a member of First Purchase Church since childhood (p.133); he worked for Dolphus Raymond as a boy, when he was severely injured (p.205); he has worked for Link Deas for eight years (p.216). But we know little about him as a person, because we only see him at the trial.

Tom is on trial for a capital charge, meaning he will be electrocuted if he's found guilty. But he's also suffering under the pressure of his segregated life. Scout, interpreting him through her own experience, doesn't realise this: for example, she thinks him polite in not striking Mayella, where Atticus later tells her that he is motivated more by sheer terror of the consequences. When he is being cross-examined by Mr Gilmer, the situation becomes more explicit.

The trial is the one time Tom speaks for himself in the novel, but everything he says is questioned, denied and reinterpreted for the jury through stereotypes about African-American men: his claiming to be innocent becomes '"being impudent"' (p.219); his generosity with his time becomes waiting for an opportunity to attack her (p.217); his feeling sorry for Mayella draws a stunned reaction from both prosecutor and crowd (p.218). Part of this is the nature of cross-examination, but behind it is an awareness of an entire system built on the negation of Tom's rights and his individuality.

Some critics, such as Monroe H Freedman (1994), have even questioned whether the account of Tom's escape attempt is really plausible, or whether his death might not have been another form of lynching. It would be over-simplification, however, to argue that Tom is not a character at all, but simply a representative for segregated and disenfranchised African-Americans as a whole.

Mayella Ewell

Key Quotes

'Mayella Ewell must have been the loneliest person in the world. She was even lonelier than Boo Radley, who had not been out of the house in twenty-five years.' (p.211)

'Tom Robinson was probably the only person who was ever decent to her. But she said he took advantage of her, and when she stood up she looked at him as if he were dirt beneath her feet.' (p.212)

Mayella is a nebulous character. Her personality and appearance are difficult to isolate: when she enters the witness stand, Scout first thinks that 'she seemed somehow fragile-looking,' but as she sits, she 'became what she was, a thick-bodied girl accustomed to strenuous labour' (p.197). Later, Jem cannot determine whether she's truly frightened, or whether '"[s]he's got enough sense to get the judge sorry for her"' (p.198). One of the puzzles of the novel is that we don't know who Mayella really is.

Mayella, like her family, is suspended uneasily between Maycomb's white community and the African-American settlement beyond town. Unlike her father and siblings, Mayella apes the conventions of the town: Scout says she 'looked as if she tried to keep clean' (p.197), and her 'six chipped-enamel slop jars holding brilliant red geraniums' (p.188) bewilder Maycomb. She has two or three years of schooling: she reads and writes to a limited degree, but cannot calculate when her mother died (p.201). Yet she remains ostracised by Maycomb, to the point where she assumes that basic Southern forms of address are 'sass' (p.200).

Atticus induces Mayella to admit that her father beats her regularly, including, by implication, the savage attack of which Tom is accused. Tom's testimony suggests that Bob also rapes his daughter: '"She says she never kissed a grown man before an's she might as well kiss a nigger. She says what her papa do to her don't count"' (p.214). This is neither addressed in court nor mentioned again in the novel.

In his summing up, Atticus talks about Mayella's 'guilt'. Certainly, she is guilty of wrongly accusing Tom. But Atticus also mentions that '"her desires were stronger than the code she was breaking"' (p.224). Even Mayella's desire for affectionate human contact is a form of guilt, despite grinding poverty and abuse. One of the unanswered questions of the novel is what will happen to Mayella and her siblings after Bob's death. The nebulous Mayella simply disappears.

Bob (Robert E. Lee) Ewell

'All the little man on the witness stand had that made him better than his nearest neighbours was that, if scrubbed with lye soap in very hot water, his skin was white.' (p.189)

'"[W]hen a man spends his relief checks on green whisky his children have a way of crying from hunger pains."' (p.34)

Bob Ewell is known to Scout and the reader by reputation long before his role in the narrative becomes clear. On her first day at school, Scout's exposure to the full range of Maycomb society includes meeting Burris Ewell, a filthy student of indeterminate age who abuses the teacher and has no intention of continuing his education. Atticus explains to Scout that the Ewells 'had been the disgrace of Maycomb for three generations' (p.33): 'They were people, but they lived like animals' (p.34). (See **Themes, Ideas & Values**.) Bob's inflated sense of his place in Maycomb society is reflected in his name's superficial but illusory connection to former Southern grandeur (Robert E. Lee was the Confederacy's top general). The Ewells are a touchstone in Maycomb society, used as a warning and an example. When Scout wants to leave school after her first day, for example, Atticus explains that she must abide by the law: the Ewells are the exception.

For Bob, Tom's trial is a crisis point. Though it does not change his underlying character, it does extend his violent behaviour outside his own family. After Atticus '"destroy[s] his last shred of credibility at that trial"' (p.241), he attacks, but never directly, anyone he feels was connected to the trial: Judge Taylor, Helen Robinson, and Atticus. Part of Bob's motivation seems to be paranoia: when he loses his WPA job, for example, he blames Atticus amid 'obscure mutterings that the bastards who thought they ran this town wouldn't permit an honest man to make a living' (p.273). Like the 'little bantam cock' (p.187) that he resembles, Bob's aggression outweighs his importance to the town.

KEY POINT

One aspect of the novel is that all characters are richly drawn and detailed. However, not all characters have a strong influence on the plot. The following characters are significant to the texture of the novel but less significant to the main plotline of the rape trial.

Calpurnia

Atticus' African-American housekeeper has the second of only two 'speaking parts' for black characters in the novel. She knows Tom Robinson's family well, and it's implied that this helps influence Atticus' decision to do his best to defend Tom (p.83). Otherwise, she has little influence on the main plot. Simultaneously affectionate and severe, Calpurnia raises Scout and Jem; this includes teaching Scout to write. She's fond of the children, but Atticus emphasises that '"she's never let them get away with anything, she's never indulged them the way most coloured nurses do"' (p.151). Despite this, some critics see her as a 'Mammy' figure (a stereotypical good-humoured, loud, slightly vulgar African-American housekeeper). Atticus considers Calpurnia as one of the family, but she remains in a subservient position: Scout's aunt, for example, forbids Scout to visit Calpurnia at home.

Miss Maudie Atkinson

Miss Maudie is an omnipresent character, but one who has little direct impact on the events of the narrative: her role is to watch and to advise. Having grown up on the neighbouring property to Finch's Landing, she's familiar enough with the family to speak with authority. Miss Maudie is liberal in outlook but politically passive (where Atticus is active). In Scout and Jem's lives, she balances the authority of Atticus (because she is outside the house and therefore objective) and Aunt Alexandra (because she is less rigid).

Dill (Charles Baker) Harris

Based on Lee's childhood friend Truman Capote, Dill is an outsider in Maycomb: he is from Mississippi; he dresses better than the other

Depression-era children and has disposable income. Dill – 'a pocket Merlin, whose head teemed with eccentric plans, strange longings, and quaint fancies' (p.8) – ignites Jem and Scout's fascination with melodrama. As a regular summer visitor, he is present for all the important moments of the novel. But he is outside what Scout calls the 'tribal groups' (p.142) of Maycomb, bringing a new perspective to the events of the insular town. Aunt Alexandra considers him cynical, though he protests, '"[t]ellin' the truth's not cynical, is it?"' (p.236). Though sensitive enough to cry at Tom's trial, he ultimately takes refuge in bitter humour: '"I'm gonna be a new kind of clown. I'm gonna stand in the middle of the ring and laugh at the folks"' (p.239).

Aunt Alexandra

Aunt Alexandra, Atticus' sister, initially appears distant: she has little interaction with her husband and apparently no real relationship with her son (p.85). The only character to whom she seems sympathetic is her grandson Francis. Scout, likening her to Mount Everest, says, 'throughout my early life, she was cold and there' (p.86). Aunt Alexandra is 'one of the last of her kind,' with 'riverboat, boarding-school manners' (p.142), a lingering remnant of the plantation families of the antebellum South. Where Dill is an outsider, Aunt Alexandra 'fitted into the world of Maycomb like a hand into a glove' (p.145). Her slow thawing shows that – despite its prejudices – Maycomb society has its good side. Scout's increasing sympathy for her aunt shows her maturing away from her childhood prejudices.

Heck Tate

Heck Tate is Sheriff of Maycomb County, a forty-two-year-old man 'as tall as Atticus, but thinner' (p.104). He appears at crisis points in the novel: the mad dog attack; before Tom's lynching; at Tom's trial; and after Bob's attack on the children. Tate claims that he's 'not a very good man' (p.303) and demonstrates Maycomb's prejudices when he paraphrases Bob's evidence as '"some nigger'd raped his girl"' (p.184). He shows a preference for an abstract justice over the law in at least one instance, when Boo attacks Bob. One question to consider regarding Tate is why he and all his men leave the jail when they know of plans to lynch Tom.

THEMES, IDEAS & VALUES

Growing up Southern

Key Quote

'Being Southerners, it was a source of shame to some members of the family that we had no recorded relatives on either side of the Battle of Hastings.' (p.3)

What it means to be Southern influences all levels of *To Kill a Mockingbird*. Southern culture remains distinct from that of other parts of the US. After their defeat in the Civil War, southern states sought to maintain the traditions of the antebellum (pre-war) South, leading to stereotypes of retributive, violent Southern men and delicate Southern belles. The South is both politically and religiously conservative: the Bible Belt, for example, runs through the South. These conventions pervade Southern literature, particularly Southern Gothic novels (see **Vocabulary**).

The very vocabulary of the novel, rich in unexplained dialect, immerses the reader in the manners of the Deep South (see vocabulary notes to **Chapter-by-Chapter Analysis**). Scout seems to be speaking to one of her compatriots. Even in the early stages of the novel, Scout shows her familiarity with the prejudices of Maycomb and writes as though the reader is also familiar with them. Describing her teacher, Miss Caroline Fisher, for example, she mentions that the class 'murmured apprehensively' (p.18) when Miss Caroline mentions that she's from Winston County in the north of the state, because every child knows that Winston County seceded from Alabama in 1861 rather than join the Confederacy: 'North Alabama was full of Liquor Interests, Big Mules, steel companies, Republicans, professors, and other persons of no background' (p.18).

Even if the reader is unaware that 'Big Mules' refers to industry executives from Birmingham (in the north of the state) or that southern states largely voted Democrat until the widespread shift to Republican in the 1960s, they appreciate that Miss Caroline is somehow foreign even though she is still from Alabama. The same is true of Misses Tutti and Frutti Barber, two women who 'were rumoured to be Republicans, having migrated from Clanton, Alabama, in 1911' (p.277); Clanton is in the middle of the state, further south than Winston County, but the Misses Barber still have 'Yankee ways' (p.277). This immersion in Southern life allows an incisive engagement with the more complicated and problematic aspects of life in the Deep South, such as segregation and institutionalised racism.

In an interview in Chicago in 1963, Lee said:

> [I]n the book I tried to give a sense of proportion to life in the South, that there isn't a lynching before every breakfast. I think that Southerners react with the same kind of horror as other people do about the injustice in their land (cited in Shields 2007 p.222).

As a result, some critics feel that Atticus' criticism of his community does not extend far enough. Certainly, Atticus is not able to help Tom Robinson, though it is unlikely that anyone could successfully have defended an African-American man on the charge of raping a white woman in a small town in the Depression-era Deep South. But when Lee explains these unpleasant aspects of small-town Southern life, she usually uses Atticus as her mouthpiece.

As Lee's statement above shows, Maycomb is in some ways a softer, gentler version of the South. Take, for example, Scout's successful disruption of the planned lynching outside Tom's jail cell. Scout first tries violence, trying to kick a man in the shin and hitting his groin instead (p.169), and then tries friendly conversation. Scout misreads the gang's purpose, finding herself facing 'the futility one feels when unacknowledged by a chance acquaintance' (p.169). The attempted lynching descends into another kind of social gathering, in which Scout tries 'a last-ditch effort to make [Mr Cunningham] feel at home' (p.169).

Later, Atticus describes the attempted lynching as a 'blind spot':

> A mob's always made up of people, no matter what. Mr Cunningham was part of a mob last night, but he was still a man. Every mob in every little Southern town is always made up of people you know (p.173).

Considering that in the early twentieth century, 'some two to three black Southerners were hanged, burned at the stake, or quietly murdered every week' (Litwack, p.20), Scout's successful intervention and Atticus' interpretation suggest that Maycomb folk are rather less bloodthirsty than some of their compatriots. Less bloodthirsty still is Atticus. Though he is not, in 1935, the kind of civil-rights activist who would risk his life in Birmingham, Alabama in the early 1960s, he represents a new breed of Southern gentleman: less vindictive, insular and bloodthirsty than his neighbours. Similarly, Scout's defusing of the situation, not through unladylike violence but through polite social conversation, shows her to be a new breed of Southern belle, not the type of 'little lady' that Aunt Alexandra wants her to be (p.147), but the new kind of 'little lady' whom Walter Cunningham recognises (p.170).

Family

KEY QUOTE

'Although Maycomb was ignored during the War Between the States, Reconstruction rule and economic ruin forced the town to grow. It grew inward.' (p.144)

In the late-nineteenth and early-twentieth centuries, US scientists were increasingly interested in eugenics (the study of selective breeding applied to people), with a view to increasing the overall health of the species. In such pre-civil rights days, the interest focused on the health of the white population, leading to laws forbidding inter-racial marriage, programmes of forced sterilisation for the 'feeble-minded' and, some argue, changes to immigration laws.

The popularity of eugenics did not wane until after the fall of Nazi Germany (whose Holocaust was a eugenics programme). *To Kill a Mockingbird* shows this 1930s' interest in the functioning of race and family. For example, once Tom has been killed, lingering sympathy in Maycomb is swallowed up in condemnation by the town majority:

> Just shows you, that Robinson was legally married, they say he kept himself clean, went to church and all that, but when it comes down to the line the veneer's mighty thin. Nigger always comes out in 'em (p.265).

Moreover, Maycomb is an inward-looking town; Scout emphasises that '[n]ew people so rarely settled there, the same families married the same families until the members of the community looked faintly alike' (p.144). (This description limits 'community' to 'white community,' excluding the African-American population.) The result, argues Scout, is that Maycomb's citizens 'were utterly predictable to one another: they took for granted attitudes, character shading, even gestures, as having been repeated in each generation and refined by time' (p.145). Maycomb is, essentially, one large family.

This aspect of Maycomb life is only brought to Scout's attention when Aunt Alexandra arrives to live with them, bringing with her a perplexing 'preoccupation with heredity' (p.143). Aunt Alexandra is vocal about her preoccupation: 'She never let a chance escape her to point out the short-comings of other tribal groups to the greater glory of our own' (p.142). Where Aunt Alexandra is essentially interested in 'tribal' differences that show the Finches to advantage, Jem encourages Scout to think in terms of family resemblances: 'Aunty better watch how she talks – scratch most folks in Maycomb and they're kin to us' (p.142).

Aunt Alexandra's purpose is to bring Scout and Jem to a sense of their social status as, in Atticus' words, '"the little lady and gentleman that you are"' (p.147). She focuses particularly on Scout, whom she feels lacks a female authority figure; Scout resists. Aunt Alexandra's intentions are not malicious, but they are unsuccessful: 'Aunt Alexandra fitted into the world of Maycomb like a hand into a glove, but never into the world of Jem and me' (p.145).

Her attempts are counteracted by Atticus' broader definition of family. Where Aunt Alexandra feels that Scout lacks a female authority figure, Atticus describes Calpurnia as '"a faithful member of this family"' (p.150). Indeed, Calpurnia is Scout's primary female influence, teaching her to write (p.20) just as Atticus taught her to read (p.19). Atticus' more inclusive notion of family tempers Aunt Alexandra's ideas.

The Radleys provide a different example: the idea that 'family' is as much about social responsibility and customs as it is about love. By the time Jem and Scout are old enough to understand, the Radleys have become a folk tale within the town (p.9). Boo's brief participation in a gang of Cunninghams is innocent enough: the gang 'did little, but enough to be discussed by the town and publicly warned from three pulpits' (p.10). Mr Radley chooses to discipline Boo himself: where the other boys are sent to industrial school – which 'was no prison and it was no disgrace' (p.11) – Boo is incarcerated in his own home, not chained to the bed as Jem supposes, but gradually turned into something akin to the phantom that the children imagine.

The entire Radley family partakes of what they see as Boo's shame: though the elder Radleys are 'welcome anywhere in town' (p.10), neither leaves the house with any regularity, Mrs Radley even forgoing the Maycomb pastime of evening visits with neighbours. Even when Boo's punishment becomes public, when he stabs his father with scissors, he is not taken to jail, but locked in the courthouse basement, an in-between space that is neither public nor private. When Mr Radley dies, his son Nathan takes his place as Boo's jailer.

Boo's return to Maycomb society is left to Scout, after he rescues her and Jem from Bob Ewell. Here Scout recognises Aunt Alexandra's teachings about social roles, as she says, 'I would lead him through our house, but I would never lead him home' (p.306). Instead of leading Boo by the hand like a child, she takes his arm: 'if Miss Stephanie Crawford was watching from her upstairs window, she would see Arthur Radley escorting me down the sidewalk, as any gentleman would do' (p.306).

Boo's position as one of Maycomb's gentlemen can only last until Scout escorts him home: Mr Radley's desperate desire to preserve his family honour has left Boo too badly damaged. But his exposure to Scout and Jem brings another result: when Scout pauses on the street corner to think back over the past two years, she uses the term 'his children'. Initially, this refers to Atticus, as when she says 'A man stood waiting with his hands on his hips' (p.307). But the term blurs until it refers to both Atticus and Boo: 'Summer, and he watched his children's hearts break. Autumn again, and Boo's children needed him' (p.308).

Though Aunt Alexandra believes that 'family' is breeding and the Radleys that 'family' is shame, Scout's experience shows 'family' as less restrictive and more welcoming.

The outsider in society

> '"There's four kinds of folks in the world. There's the ordinary kind like us and the neighbours, there's the kind like the Cunninghams out in the woods, the kind like the Ewells down at the dump, and the Negroes."' (p.249)

Outsider status in Maycomb society is not only a matter of race. Despite it being an insular town, most of its inhabitants are outsiders in some way: Miss Maudie, for example, is a Baptist at odds with the 'foot-washing Baptists,' who 'believe anything that's pleasure is a sin' (p.49), including Miss Maudie's flowers; and Dill Harris is 'a curiosity' in his 'blue linen shorts that buttoned to his shirt' (p.8) compared to Scout's Depression-era schoolmates, 'the ragged, denim-shirted and floursack-skirted first grade' (p.18). The broadest example of this type of outsider is Boo Radley, whose minor transgression against the town's mores – not only charges of assault and battery and disorderly conduct but also 'using abusive and profane language in the presence and hearing of a female' (p.11) – leads to his imprisonment.

However, these characters are all ultimately accepted by the community – even Boo Radley, whom the older town citizens (primarily Atticus, Miss Maudie and Heck Tate) defend not only from a charge of murder but also from the minor disrespect of being called 'Boo' instead of the traditional Southern 'Mr Arthur'. The social outsider is more noticeable in extreme cases, particularly Mr Dolphus Raymond and the Ewells.

Mr Dolphus is an outsider because he drinks and lives with an African-American woman, by whom he has several children. (Alabama enacted a ban on inter-racial marriages in 1901 and did not declare the ban illegal until the 1970s.) When Jem explains this to Dill, Dill replies, '"He doesn't look like trash"' (p.177). As Jem points out, Mr Dolphus doesn't meet Maycomb's criteria for 'trash': '"he owns all one side of the river bank down there, and he's from a real old family to boot"' (p.177).

As Scout and Dill learn during the trial, this outsider status is exaggerated: he is a sober man who presents himself as an alcoholic. To Scout, he explains that this is for Maycomb's benefit: it provides them with a reason for his defiance of custom when 'they could never, never understand that I live like I do because that's the way I want to live' (p.221). Even the young Scout – who, Mr Dolphus says, hasn't 'even seen enough of the world yet' (p.222) – is confused; she describes Mr Dolphus as a 'sinful man who had mixed race children' even while she's fascinated by 'a being who deliberately perpetrated fraud against himself' (p.221). Mr Dolphus' place in the novel suggests that Scout understands his fraud after seeing more of the world.

Unlike Mr Dolphus, who isolates himself *from* Maycomb society, the Ewells are isolated *by* Maycomb society. Scout compares Mayella Ewell not to Mr Dolphus, but to Mr Dolphus' mixed-race children:

> She was as sad, I thought, as what Jem called a mixed child: white people wouldn't have anything to do with her because she lived among pigs; Negroes wouldn't have anything to do with her because she was white. She couldn't live like Mr Dolphus Raymond, who preferred the company of Negroes, because she didn't own a riverbank and she wasn't from a fine old family (pp.211–12).

The Ewells are geographically isolated from Maycomb, living outside the dump, where they are socially suspended between the town and the African-American community. Mayella is even isolated from Maycomb's basic Southern courtesies, reacting as though her being called 'Miss Mayella' is intended as sarcasm (p.201). This isolation is not the town's response to the alcoholic, abusive Bob Ewell only: Atticus tells Scout that '"the Ewells had been the disgrace of Maycomb for three generations"' (p.33). Their isolation crosses multiple generations, until they are 'members of an exclusive society made up of Ewells' (p.34).

Despite their extreme outsider status, the Ewells can reintegrate themselves when necessary. Atticus explains to Scout early in the novel that the Ewells are exempt from some laws: the children do not have to attend school and Bob Ewell can hunt and trap out of season, though this 'misdemeanour at law' is 'a capital felony in the eyes of the populace' (p.34). For a true capital felony, however, the Ewells expect the town that scorns them to support them. As Mayella demonstrates after her flawed testimony, she need only raise the question of race: '"That nigger yonder took advantage of me, an' if you fine fancy gentlemen don't want to do nothin' about it then you're all yellow stinkin' cowards"' (p.207).

As a white woman in a society in which the races are legally and socially segregated, Mayella's isolation still allows her to claim the protection of the broader community, something to which Tom Robinson is not entitled.

Race vs. justice

Key Quotes

'"In our courts, when it's a white man's word against a black man's, the white man always wins. They're ugly, but those are the facts of life."' (p. 243)

'Tom was a dead man the minute Mayella Ewell opened her mouth and screamed' (p.266).

After *To Kill a Mockingbird*'s publication, readers wondered whether Lee was fictionalising a specific court case in Tom Robinson's trial. Charles Shields, for example, suggests she may have used the case of Walter Lett, accused of raping a white woman in 1933 near Lee's hometown of Monroeville (Shields 2007 pp.118–20). Most commonly, critics mention the Scottsboro boys: nine African-American teenagers (aged thirteen to nineteen) accused of raping two white women on a train in Scottsboro, Alabama in 1931. Asked about the Scottsboro case in 1999, Lee replied that while not thinking of it specifically, 'it will more than do as an example (albeit a lurid one) of deep-South attitudes on race vs. justice that prevailed at the time' (cited in Shields 2007 p.118).

Tom's trial exposes the operation of 'Negro law' in the Deep South. As Leon F. Litwack argues:

> Unwritten, based on experience and custom, 'Negro' law applied to much of the South. Police officers, judges, lawyers, and jurors understood that in the daily enforcement of the law, some statutes applied to both races, some only to whites, some only to blacks (Litwack 2009 p.18).

The legal system dismissed crimes within African-American communities as 'Negro affrays' (Garton 2003 p.677), but dealt severely with African-Americans accused of crimes against white people or property, if the accused did not fall victim to the white lynch mobs that 'combined the roles of judge, jury, and executioner' (Litwack 2009 p.19). In addition, courts 'excluded blacks from juries, disregarded black testimony, and meted out sentences based less on the evidence than on the race of the defendant' (Litwack 2009 p.18).

In discussing Tom's conviction, Atticus foregrounds the problem of 'Negro law', though he does not use this term. Jem struggles with Tom's death sentence, even though rape is a capital offence in Alabama: '"the jury didn't have to give him death – if they wanted to they could've gave him twenty years"' (p.242). But as Atticus argues, the sentence is (in Litwack's terms) based not on evidence but on race: '"Tom Robinson's a coloured man, Jem. No jury in this part of the world's going to say, 'We think you're guilty, but not very,' on a charge like that. It was either straight acquittal or nothing"' (p.242). The 'nothing', Atticus implies, was always the more likely outcome than acquittal.

Jem is dissatisfied with a jury-based system: '"No, sir, they oughta do away with juries. He wasn't guilty in the first place and they said he was"' (p.243). Atticus, when he defends juries, is circumspect: he mentions that women cannot serve on juries (p.244), but not that black men cannot. However, he raises a more problematic issue:

> Those are twelve reasonable men in everyday life, Tom's jury,
> but you saw something come between them and reason. You
> saw the same thing that night in front of the jail. When that
> crew went away, they didn't go as reasonable men, they went
> because we were there (p.243).

In this quote, Atticus connects the jury to the lynch mob. In doing so, he draws out the limited options available to Tom in the legal system: once accused of raping a white woman, he would die, either at the hands of the mob or under the sentence of the court.

As Stephen Garton (2003 p.690) writes,

The majority of African Americans accused of crimes faced a very harsh reality. Some were lynched and many others brought before the courts where they were convicted and sentenced to long terms working on county chain and highway gangs.

Five hundred prisoners escaped Georgia's prison system annually in the 1920s and 1930s in an attempt to flee the severity of the chain gang (Garton 2003 p.696). For Tom, escape is not an option; his attempt to scale the prison fence is futile not only because of his crippled arm, but also because, as a family man with strong ties to the community, 'a faithful member of First Purchase since he was a boy' (p.133), he has nowhere to run.

However, not all of Maycomb supports the unspoken 'Negro law'. When Jem asks Miss Maudie, '"Who in this town did one thing to help Tom Robinson, just who?"', Miss Maudie replies:

> His coloured friends for one thing, and people like us. People like Judge Taylor. People like Mr Heck Tate. Stop eating and start thinking, Jem. Did it ever strike you that Judge Taylor naming Atticus to defend that boy was no accident? That Judge Taylor might have had his reasons for naming him? (p.238).

As Scout reflects, the case would normally have been given to the youngest member of the bar, 'who needed the experience' (p.238); in a trial with an assured outcome, experience comes without pressure. Miss Maudie is not the only person to see this; Bob Ewell targets Judge Taylor after the trial. Nevertheless, Tom's fate rests on a question of race, not justice.

Tom is in contrast to Boo Radley. Both Tom and Boo are compared to the mockingbird, which it is a sin to kill. But when Boo kills Bob Ewell, the town authorities (represented by Heck Tate and Atticus) close ranks around him. Boo, unlike Tom and Bob Ewell, is from one of Maycomb's respectable white families. Sheriff Tate tells Atticus,

> … maybe you'll say it's my duty to tell the town all about it, and not hush it up. Know what'd happen then? All the ladies in

Maycomb includin' my wife'd be knocking on his door bringing angel food cake (p.304).

Tate protects the shy Boo from both the rigours of a trial and the town's gratitude. The cover-up of his crime is a sharp counterpoint to Tom's sufferings under the South's unspoken 'Negro law'.

Bravery

Key Quote

'It was times like this when I thought my father, who hated guns and had never been to any wars, was the bravest man who ever lived' (p.111).

Lee presents two opposed examples of bravery back-to-back at the end of Part One, just before Tom Robinson's trial dominates the narrative: the episodes involving the mad dog and Mrs Dubose.

The mad-dog incident comes just as Scout and Jem are beginning to worry that Atticus' age 'reflected on his abilities and manliness' (p.98). Scout, in particular, compares her father to her schoolmates' fathers, and concludes that Atticus doesn't do 'anything':

> Atticus did not drive a dump-truck for the county, he was not
> the sheriff, he did not farm, work in a garage, or do anything
> that could possibly arouse the admiration of anyone (p.99).

Because Atticus' work – both as a lawyer and in the legislature at Montgomery – is abstract rather than practical, Scout struggles to see its value until Tom's trial.

The incident of the mad dog (Chapter 10) comes at a time when Scout is particularly uncomfortable with her father's position. This is partly because Tom's coming trial makes Atticus conspicuous – which in Scout's eyes highlights his differences from other fathers – and partly because she has 'committed [herself] to a policy of cowardice' on Atticus' behalf, promising not to fight when he is insulted (p.99).

Tim Johnson's slow progress down the street is one of the most vivid scenes in the book: Lee emphasises the emptiness of the street (where the only moving figures are Atticus and Tim) and the silence (when Scout can hear her father's glasses crack when they hit the street). The menace comes from the tendency of rabid animals to become uncharacteristically aggressive and attack without provocation: as soon as Atticus is in Tim's line of sight, he is at risk.

Tim Johnson's rabies can be read as a metaphor for the town's endemic racism: in the preceding chapter (Chapter 9), Atticus says to his brother, '[w]hy reasonable people go stark raving mad when anything involving a Negro comes up, is something I don't pretend to understand' (p.98). As such, Tim stands in for Tom Robinson: Tim, shot by Atticus, dies because of an untreatable disease, just as Tom, killed by prison guards, dies because of the social madness of racism. Atticus stands between Tom and the rabid town just as he stands between the rabid Tim and the town.

In the following chapter (Chapter 11), Atticus presents Mrs Dubose as a different example of bravery. After Jem destroys Mrs Dubose's camellias, he is forced to read to her as penance. He and Scout are subjected to her abuse not only of Atticus, particularly his decision to defend Tom, but also of them. Only after her death does Atticus reveal that she was addicted to morphine, which she had been prescribed as a painkiller. Jem's punishment at her hands is, Atticus says, also a lesson in bravery: 'I wanted you to see what real courage is, instead of getting the idea that courage is a man with a gun in his hand' (p.124). He describes Mrs Dubose as a 'great lady', despite the fact that '[s]he had her own view of things, a lot different from mine, maybe' (p.124). This, the final incident of Part One, is a further example of Atticus resisting traditional Southern codes of courage.

If Part One ends with an example of bravery, Part Two ends with an example of cowardice: Bob Ewell's attempt to kill Scout and Jem. Ewell's cowardice comes from his desire to use his power to overcome the powerless. Where Atticus, in Miss Maudie's words, '"put his gun down when he realized that God had given him an unfair advantage over most living things"' (p.109), Ewell is Atticus' counter example: the man who feels brave when he has a weapon in his hand.

DIFFERENT INTERPRETATIONS

Different interpretations arise from different responses to a text. Over time, a text will give rise to a wide range of responses from its readers, who may come from various social or cultural groups and live in very different places and historical periods. These responses can be published in newspapers, journals and books by critics and reviewers, or they can be expressed in discussions among readers in the media, classrooms, book groups and so on. While there is no single correct reading or interpretation of a text, it is important to understand that an interpretation is more than a personal opinion – it is the justification of a point of view on the text. To present an interpretation of the text based on your point of view you must use a logical argument and support it with relevant evidence from the text.

The critics' viewpoints

To Kill a Mockingbird is one of the most widely sold and widely read books of the twentieth century, frequently set on school reading lists and almost as frequently banned from libraries. However, as Alice Hall Petry points out, '[o]ne also would be hard pressed to think of a novel as successful, honored (including the Pulitzer Prize), and respected as *Mockingbird* that has received such modest attention from the academic community' (Petry 2008 p.*vx*).

Part of the problem may lie in the fact the criticism of the novel occupies an uneasy space between the past and the present. Just as the novel hovers between 1933–5 and 1960, critics hover between then and now. The glowing early reviews of the novel are a useful way for a modern reader to understand its immediate impact (see, for example, Shields for an excellent range of contemporary reviews). But after 1965, the Civil Rights Movement so changed the social landscape that, as Petry argues, 'It is perhaps impossible for students and scholars born after around 1955 to appreciate what a groundbreaking, even *shocking* book *To Kill a Mockingbird* seemed in the early 1960s' (Petry 2008 p.*xxiii*).

However, if scholars interpret the novel in the light of modern social codes, they risk falling into the trap of presentism (an analytical method that anachronistically introduces modern modes of behaviour into past works). This uneasy critical space is represented in debates over the banning of the work: do we, for example, accept that Lee uses and critiques the word 'nigger' as an aspect of the 1930s' Deep South, or do we argue that twenty-first-century students will find the word aggressive and distressing? Scholars of the novel need to consider both these perspectives.

An intriguing aspect of *Mockingbird* scholarship is that after the initial publication, it was lawyers who took over from the reviewers, not literary scholars. As Claudia Durst Johnson points out, 'since 1960 a greater volume of critical readings of the novel has been amassed by two legal scholars in law journals than by all the literary scholars in literary journals' (Johnson, p.20). Both the *Alabama Law Review* (in 1994) and the *Michigan Law Review* (in 1999) have devoted whole sections (in the former instance, the entire issue) to analysing the novel. The impetus for this is Atticus Finch. In Steven Lubet's terms, 'No real-life lawyer has done more for the self-image or public perception of the legal profession than the hero of Harper Lee's novel' (Lubet 1999 p.1339).

Not all lawyers' responses to Atticus are positive. In 1992, Monroe H Freedman initiated a flurry of debate when he published two articles in the *Legal Times* suggesting that Atticus was no model for a modern lawyer. Freedman revisited his argument in 1994's 'Atticus Finch – Right and Wrong,' in which he argues that Atticus 'knows about the grinding, ever-present humiliation and degradation of the black people of Maycomb; he tolerates it; and sometimes he even trivializes and condones it' (Freedman 1994 p.479). While Freedman's argument has its own flaws, it has had a significant impact on scholarly assessment of the novel. As Petry argues, 'If nothing else, Freedman's unpopular reassessment of Atticus Finch has led to a reassessment of his conduct as both a lawyer and a citizen of Maycomb' (Petry 2008 p.xxvii). Lawyers' criticisms of the novel need to be used cautiously; though insightful and detailed, they come from a discipline entirely different from literary scholarship.

Literary scholarship built slowly: the first full-length study of the novel, Claudia Durst Johnson's *To Kill a Mockingbird: Threatening Boundaries*, was published in 1994 and the first collection of essays, Alice Hall Petry's *On Harper Lee*, did not appear until 2007. Perhaps because *Mockingbird* is comparatively new to the academy, the material appearing covers a wide range of approaches to the text.

Like the lawyers, literary scholars consider the question of Atticus' role in the novel, as when Joseph Crespino analyses Atticus as both a Southern liberal and a man of his time, arguing that Lee's characters 'reflect the moral tensions that all liberals faced in the Jim Crow Deep South' (Crespino 2000 p.14). Critics also explore textual angles that are the traditional province of literary studies: the success of Scout's dual narrative voices and the repression of other voices; religion's place in the novel; the novel's critique of Southern identity; or Lee's use of Gothic tropes such as the seemingly haunted house.

Though literary criticism of the novel is surprisingly sparse, the existing material is rich and varied. For a comprehensive and intelligent analytical survey of scholarship up to 2007, see Alice Hall Petry's introduction to *On Harper Lee*.

The following represent two different ways of analysing *To Kill a Mockingbird*.

1. Ultimately, *To Kill a Mockingbird* is a book with a happy ending.

In chapter one of *To Kill a Mockingbird*, Dill Harris bets that Jem Finch 'wouldn't get any farther than the Radley gate' (p.14), an action that Dill hopes will provoke Boo Radley into coming out of the house. Later, the bet is reduced to '"just go up and touch the house"' (p.16). Jem duly 'sped up to the side of the house, slapped it with his palm and ran back to us' (p.16). The bet is won; the prize is handed over. The prize is a copy of Robert F. Schulkers' *Stoner's Boy; or, the Mystery of the Gray Ghost* (1926), the fourth in Schulkers' popular series about the adventures of a rotating cast of boys protecting their riverbank clubhouse.

In the final chapter of the novel, after Scout has escorted Boo Radley home, she walks into Jem's bedroom. Jem is sedated following Bob Ewell's attack, with a broken arm that is permanently damaged. Atticus sits by Jem's bed, reading *The Gray Ghost*. Scout asks that he read it out loud, because "[i]t's real scary' (p.308). She sleeps as Atticus reads, and when he wakes her, gives her own version of the story:

> An' they chased him 'n' never could catch him 'cause they didn't know what he looked like, an' Atticus, when they finally saw him, why he hadn't done any of those things … Atticus, he was real nice' (p.309).

Atticus replies, '"Most people are, Scout, when you finally see them"' (p.309), and the novel ends.

Is Scout's sleepy re-telling of *The Gray Ghost* an accurate synopsis? It doesn't matter. *To Kill a Mockingbird* is a circular narrative: it begins and ends with Jem's broken arm. *The Gray Ghost* reiterates that circular structure: it begins the novel as an item of exchange in the children's games with Boo Radley, and it ends the novel as a way for nine-year-old Scout to understand her changing perception of Boo.

The early chapters of the novel are haunted by the 'malevolent phantom' Boo Radley, who 'went out at night when the moon was high' (p.9), peeping in windows, killing pets and freezing flowers with his icy breath. Scout, Jem, and Dill are in turn fascinated with him and terrified of him, alternately sneaking up to his windows or running past his house in case he grabs them. In the final chapters of the novel, Boo Radley does come out of his house. On a night when '[t]here was no moon' (p.280), he leaves the house he has left only a handful of times (each on Scout and Jem's behalf) in the past twenty-five years, and saves two children from the violence of a drunken, vengeful man. Though he never leaves the house again, the malevolent phantom is laid to rest. Boo, as Scout knows, 'hadn't done any of those things'.

The novel's circular narrative does not negate the terrible events of the novel itself: Mayella's beating, Tom's trial, Jem's injury and Bob's death all still take place. But the circular narrative encloses them. It draws Scout and the reader back to the sleepy, insular Maycomb of the beginning, but a Maycomb filtered through Scout's new perceptiveness. *To Kill a Mockingbird* ends where it begins, where, to Scout, 'nothin's real scary except in books' (p.309).

2. *To Kill a Mockingbird* is a novel whose tragedies are hidden by a superficially happy ending.

To Kill a Mockingbird ends with Atticus tucking Scout into bed and telling her that most people are nice '"when you finally see them"' (p.309). But the tragedies of *To Kill a Mockingbird* lie in what we do not see. Teresa Godwin Phelps argues that, apart from racism, 'there is another disease in Maycomb that Atticus does not see: the disease of marginalization' (Phelps 1994 p.514). The marginalised, tragic characters of the novel are non-narratable: they are the ones whose endings are forgotten or who have no endings at all.

Of these characters, perhaps the most apparent is Tom Robinson. Tom appears in person for his trial, where his every word is questioned and filtered through Maycomb's racism. He is, in his every appearance, already a ghost: in Scout's terms, 'Tom was a dead man the minute Mayella Ewell opened her mouth and screamed' (p.266). When he dies, it is away from the reader's eyes; his death is narrated by another character, as is his widow's grief.

After his death, he is further erased. Atticus, trying to ease his children's trauma, tells them that 'after enough time passed people would forget that Tom Robinson's existence was ever brought to their attention' (p.268). And they do: 'Maycomb was interested in the news of Tom's death for perhaps two days' (p.265). When Scout later says of Bob Ewell that he 'found himself as forgotten as Tom Robinson' (p.273), the phrase is as familiar as a proverb. Tom's lasting legacy is how easily he disappears. By the end of the novel, Tom lingers only in the fact that Jem's broken 'left arm was somewhat shorter than his right' (p.3), an echo of the disability that indicated Tom's innocence. As Phelps argues, '[t]he bitter truth that flies in the face of all interpretations that see triumph in the book is that

Tom Robinson is dead' (Phelps 1994 p.529), no matter how far the book shies from narrating this death.

Yet Tom's end is still more narratable than that of Mayella Ewell. Like Tom, Mayella's ability to speak for herself is constrained. In part, this is because the reader is encouraged to accept that she is perjuring herself at the trial: even when she speaks, the narrative tells us, she is lying. What the novel does not interrogate is why she lies. In trying to demonstrate Tom's innocence, Atticus' summing-up emphasises Mayella's guilt. Her crime, says Atticus, is conscious, because '"she was no child hiding stolen contraband: she struck out at her victim"' (p.224).

Mayella, too, is a victim. Atticus calls her a '"victim of cruel poverty and ignorance"' (p.224). Maycomb, however, is complicit in Mayella's victimisation. For example, Atticus explains to Scout early in the novel that '"[t]here are ways of keeping people in school by force, but it's silly to force people like the Ewells into a new environment"' (p.34). Maycomb, it seems, sees no exceptions where the rule of the Ewells is concerned.

Similarly, Tom's testimony reveals horrifying details about Mayella's home life. Under oath, he repeats Mayella's words to him: '"She says she never kissed a grown man before an's she might as well kiss a nigger. She says what her papa do to her don't count"' (p.214). Like the savage beating that someone, if not Tom, gave Mayella, the incestuous rape is never mentioned again in the novel. Nor does anyone in the novel question what will happen to the now-orphaned Ewells after Bob is killed.

If Tom's tragedy is that his ending is swiftly forgotten, Mayella's tragedy is that she has no ending at all. In Phelps' words, the Ewells 'have been used to develop the plot and explicate the conflict and then tossed back on the dump' (Phelps 1994 p.526). To Kill a Mockingbird's marginalised characters remain marginalised to the end.

QUESTIONS & ANSWERS

This section focuses on your own analytical writing on the text, and gives you strategies for producing high quality responses in your coursework and exam essays.

Essay writing – an overview

An essay is a formal and serious piece of writing that presents your point of view on the text, usually in response to a given essay topic. Your 'point of view' in an essay is your interpretation of the meaning of the text's language, structure, characters, situations and events, supported by detailed analysis of textual evidence.

Analyse – don't summarise

In your essays it is important to avoid simply summarising what happens in a text:

- A summary is a description or paraphrase (retelling in different words) of the characters and events. For example: 'Macbeth has a horrifying vision of a dagger dripping with blood before he goes to murder King Duncan'.

- An analysis is an explanation of the real meaning or significance that lies 'beneath' the text's words (and images, for a film). For example: 'Macbeth's vision of a bloody dagger shows how deeply uneasy he is about the violent act he is contemplating – as well as his sense that supernatural forces are impelling him to act'.

- A limited amount of summary is sometimes necessary to let your reader know which part of the text you wish to discuss. However, always keep this to a minimum and follow it immediately with your analysis (explanation) of what this part of the text is really telling us.

Plan your essay

Carefully plan your essay so that you have a clear idea of what you are going to say. The plan ensures that your ideas flow logically, that your argument remains consistent and that you stay on the topic. An essay plan should be a list of **brief dot points** – no more than half a page. It includes:

- your central argument or main contention – a concise statement (usually in a single sentence) of your overall response to the topic. See 'Analysing a sample topic' for guidelines on how to formulate a main contention.

- three or four dot points for each paragraph indicating the main idea and evidence/examples from the text. Note that in your essay you will need to expand on these points and analyse the evidence.

Structure your essay

An essay is a complete, self-contained piece of writing. It has a clear beginning (the introduction), middle (several body paragraphs) and end (the last paragraph or conclusion). It must also have a central argument that runs throughout, linking each paragraph to form a coherent whole.

See examples of introductions and conclusions in the 'Analysing a sample topic' and 'Sample answer' sections.

The introduction establishes your overall response to the topic. It includes your main contention and outlines the main evidence you will refer to in the course of the essay. Write your introduction after you have done a plan and before you write the rest of the essay.

The body paragraphs argue your case – they present evidence from the text and explain how this evidence supports your argument. Each body paragraph needs:

- a strong **topic sentence** (usually the first sentence) that states the main point being made in the paragraph

- **evidence** from the text, including some brief quotations

- **analysis** of the textual evidence explaining its significance and explanation of how it supports your argument

- **links back to the topic** in one or more statements, usually towards the end of the paragraph.

Connect the body paragraphs so that your discussion flows smoothly. Use some linking words and phrases like 'similarly' and 'on the other hand', though don't start every paragraph like this. Another strategy is to use a significant word from the last sentence of one paragraph in the first sentence of the next.

Use key terms from the topic – or similes for them – throughout, so the relevance of your discussion to the topic is always clear.

The conclusion ties everything together and finishes the essay. It includes strong statements that emphasise your central argument and provide a clear response to the topic.

Avoid simply restating the points made earlier in the essay – this will end on a very flat note and imply that you have run out of ideas and vocabulary. The conclusion is meant to be a logical extension of what you have written, not just a repetition or summary of it. Writing an effective conclusion can be a challenge. Try using these tips:

- Start by linking back to the final sentence of the second-last paragraph – this helps your writing to 'flow', rather than just leaping back to your main contention straight away.

- Use similes and expressions with equivalent meanings to vary your vocabulary. This allows you to reinforce your line of argument without being repetitive.

- When planning your essay, think of one or two broad statements or observations about the text's wider meaning. These should be related to the topic and your overall argument. Keep them for the conclusion, since they will give you something 'new' to say but still follow logically from your discussion. The introduction will be focused on the topic, but the conclusion can present a wider view of the text.

Essay topics

1 '[T]he book's central meanings can be accessed most readily by exploring Lee's religious vision' (Robert Butler). What role does religion play in *To Kill a Mockingbird*?

2 '"I've thought about it a lot lately and I've got it figured out. There's four kinds of folks in the world ..."'
'"Naw, Jem, I think there's just one kind of folks. Folks."' Do you agree with Jem or with Scout?

3 'Lee's problem has been to tell the story she wants to tell and yet to stay within the consciousness of a child, and she hasn't consistently solved it' (Granville Hicks). Do you agree?

4 'Atticus Finch is the same in his house as he is on the public streets.' Discuss.

5 'You never really understand a person until you consider things from his point of view ... until you climb into his skin and walk around in it.' Discuss.

6 '*To Kill a Mockingbird* is unable to come to any real conclusions about the problems of race in the Deep South.' Discuss.

7 'Ladies seemed to live in faint horror of men, seemed unwilling to approve wholeheartedly of them. But I liked them.' What does *To Kill a Mockingbird* say about gender?

8 What role does the Gothic play in *To Kill a Mockingbird*?

9 '*To Kill a Mockingbird* is a novel about growing up.' Discuss.

10 'No character in the novel is free from the societal disease of racism.' Discuss.

Vocabulary for writing on *To Kill a Mockingbird*

To Kill a Mockingbird is not a technically complex novel, but the following terms are valuable when analysing it.

Antebellum: used generally to mean a pre-war period, but used specifically in the US to describe pre-Civil War Southern culture. Lee uses antebellum archetypes (such as the importance of family) to critique them (as in the punishment of Boo).

Bildungsroman: literally translated from German as 'novel of formation,' a *Bildungsroman* is a coming-of-age story, recounting a character's psychological and physical development from childhood to an adult sense of the world. Famous examples of *Bildungsroman* include Charles Dickens' *Great Expectations* (1860–1), L.M. Montgomery's *Anne of Green Gables* (1908), and J.D. Salinger's *The Catcher in the Rye* (1951).

Picaresque: literary technique that recounts the episodic adventures of a rogue or anti-hero. Though Scout is not an anti-hero, the misleadingly disconnected episodes of Part One can be seen as picaresque. A famous example of this use of the device is Mark Twain's *The Adventures of Huckleberry Finn* (1885), where Huck's varied adventures are only connected by the motif of the river.

Southern Gothic: uniquely American sub-genre of Gothic literature. Traditional Gothic literature combines romance and horror, relying on supernatural (or apparently supernatural) events for its plots. Southern Gothic manipulates the archetypes of traditional Gothic literature (such as the persecuted woman) and of Southern literature (such as the Southern belle) to create morbid, grotesque, or tragic critiques of the South. Famous Southern Gothic writers include Truman Capote, William Faulkner, and Flannery O'Connor. Only recently has Southern Gothic relied on strongly paranormal content (for example, Anne Rice's novels).

Southern literature (or Literature of the American South): broadly, literature from or about the southern US, which emerged as a distinct category after the American War of Independence. Southern literature uses uniquely Southern dialects and questions issues of shared Southern history (the Civil War, post-war Reconstruction, and cultural separation from the North); family and community; and race relations (slavery and civil rights tensions). Southern literature can be divided into antebellum literature (such as Harriet Beecher Stowe's *Uncle Tom's Cabin*); post-Civil War literature (such as Mark Twain's novels); and novels of the 'Southern Renaissance,' which began in the 1920s (such as Margaret Mitchell's *Gone with the Wind* and Tennessee Williams' *A Streetcar Named Desire*).

Unreliable narrator: a narrator whose accuracy and truthfulness is questionable. An unreliable narrator might be mentally ill (as in Ken Kesey's *One Flew Over the Cuckoo's Nest*); might be deceiving the reader (as in Agatha Christie's *The Murder of Roger Ackroyd*), or seeking the reader's sympathy (as in Vladimir Nabokov's *Lolita*). Child narrators are often categorised as unreliable simply because of their youth, especially when narrating socially complex events.

Analysing a sample topic

This section leads you through the analysis of a single topic and the planning of a response.

'No character in the novel is free from the societal disease of racism'. Discuss.

The question's key terms are 'no character', 'free', 'racism', and 'societal disease'. 'No character' assumes that all characters are, to some degree, racist. 'Free' is a complicated term: it does not imply that all characters are hysterical bigots, merely that racism influences all characters to some degree. 'Racism' itself is a term that requires consideration: think about what racism means in the context of the novel. In conjunction with 'free', the term 'racism' becomes more complicated: a character might not be racist and yet still might not be free from racism if their entire lives are constrained by it. The final key term asks you to address whether *Mockingbird* constructs racism as a disease and, moreover, a disease that is transmitted through and across society.

Note that the question is constructed as a statement. It assumes that all characters in the novel are racist to some degree. To answer this question effectively, either agree with this statement in its totality or make a case for some characters being free from racism. To merely discuss either racist or non-racist characters would not fully answer this question.

An outline of a sample answer to this question is given below. This outline is only one possible way of answering the question.

Introduction:

To Kill a Mockingbird constructs racism as a disease that infects all layers of Maycomb society. To show racism as a disease, Lee links the episode of the mad dog to Tom Robinson's coming trial. The trial itself reveals a deep underlying racism in Maycomb society, culminating in an attempted lynching. Even the novel's admirable characters, such as Atticus, are not entirely free from this disease. In a slightly different form, racism is also evident within Maycomb's African-American community. Of all the novel's characters, only Jem seems to give hope that he will not be infected, suggesting that racism might not be as pervasive a disease as the novel fears.

Paragraph One: *To Kill a Mockingbird* constructs racism as a disease.

- Atticus' quotations, that he hopes his children will be free from '"Maycomb's usual disease"' and that '"reasonable people go stark raving mad when anything involving a Negro comes up"' (p.98), reflect the topic's key terms.

- Introduce the incident with the rabid dog.

- Analyse the image of the rabid dog as a metaphor for racism. Think closely about the metaphor's effectiveness: rabies is highly contagious, fatal once the symptoms show, and makes the sufferer extremely dangerous to others.

Paragraph Two: Tom's trial reveals a deep underlying racism in Maycomb.

- Analyse the racial invective in the novel: even before the trial begins, the reader hears Maycomb's citizens use highly pejorative terms to describe African-Americans.

- Analyse the town's feeling about the trial, from Cecil Jacob's claim that '"that nigger oughta hang from the water-tank"' (p.85) to Mrs Dubose's attacks on the children and Atticus.

- Conclude with the attempted lynching of Tom, the most dramatic and violent outpouring of racism in the novel. A good quote to use here is Atticus saying, '"A mob's always made up of people, no matter what"' (p.173), because it reinforces the idea of racism being contagious.

Paragraph Three: Even admirable characters are not entirely free from racism.

- Introduce Scout's use of racial invective, especially 'nigger,' even though she is otherwise a sympathetic character.

- The most powerful example is Atticus, because he is the most upright character in the novel.

- Give examples where Atticus' attitude is questionable: his admission that he didn't take Tom's case voluntarily (p.98) and his claim that the Ku Klux Klan was 'a political organization more than anything' (p.161).

- Conclude by limiting the argument: Atticus is not racist as, for example, the lynch mob is racist, but he is not entirely free from the disease.

Paragraph Four: Racism is also evident in Maycomb's African-American community.

- The key example here is Lula, the black separatist who objects to Scout and Jem attending First Purchase (Chapter 12).

- Provide examples of Lula's racism: her objection to white children in an African-American space, her distaste for Calpurnia working as a servant in a white household.

- As with the previous paragraph, show the limits of this argument: positioning Lula's racism as a response to white hatred and violence will give you a more nuanced argument.

Paragraph Five: Jem is one character who might not be infected with Maycomb's disease.

- Outline Jem's sensitivity to racial issues.

- Give specific examples: Jem talks sympathetically about mixed-race children, about mixed marriages, and the nebulous nature of white identity (p.177–8).

- Analyse Jem's traumatised reaction to the trial and dissatisfaction with Atticus' measured responses about the law and due process.

Conclusion:

Tom Robinson's trial brings an outpouring of racial invective and racially motivated violence to Maycomb, suggesting that, like the rabies that killed Tim Johnson, racism is easily transmitted and fatal. Even Atticus, perhaps the most morally upright character in the novel, seems not entirely immune. But Jem's experiences suggest that the younger generation might not be as susceptible to the disease of racism as their parents.

SAMPLE ANSWER

'Ladies seemed to live in faint horror of men, seemed unwilling to approve wholeheartedly of them. But I liked them.' What does *To Kill a Mockingbird* say about gender?

The central gender issue in *To Kill a Mockingbird* is whether Scout Finch will cast off her tomboyish ways and become a Southern lady. Scout begins the novel by resisting the traditional feminine values of her upbringing. As the novel progresses, more pressure is brought on her to conform to the ideals of Southern womanhood. But the novel also critiques these ideals and shows them to be a mask for secret vices and unpleasantness. In the end, the novel reaches a compromise, where Scout and Southern womanhood meet each other halfway.

In the early chapters of the novel, Scout resists the traditional feminine values and practices that she sees around her in Maycomb. These values are about constraint: the 'ladies wore corsets,' bathed twice a day, and in hot weather 'were like soft tea-cakes with frostings of sweat and sweet talcum'. The missionary tea later in the novel shows the reader that Southern femininity is about external appearances: 'fragile pastel prints,' face powder but no rouge, natural nail polishes, highly scented perfumes. Scout resists all this. Instead, she fights, speaks up in class, wears overalls, socialises exclusively with boys and plays football. The tomboyish Scout, in the early chapters, could not be further from the fragile, pastel, delicately scented women of Maycomb.

As Scout grows up, her tomboyish ways become more of a concern to her relatives, and increasing pressure is brought on her to conform. The main source of pressure is her Aunt Alexandra. Aunt Alexandra, with her 'riverboat, boarding-school manners', is the epitome of Southern womanhood in the novel. She fits into the traditional feminine world of Maycomb 'like a hand into a glove,' a simile that reinforces the ideal of Southern women as detached and protected from contact with dirt. Aunt Alexandra wants Scout to be 'a ray of sunshine'. But her idea of sunshine is limited to toy tea sets and jewellery. Living with Aunt Alexandra restricts Scout's freedom, especially as Atticus seems sympathetic to his sister's endeavours.

But even as Scout is pressured to conform, the novel critiques the ideals of Southern womanhood. With the possible exception of Miss Maudie, Maycomb's women have secret vices: Mrs Dubose is a morphine addict, Miss Rachel drinks a glass of neat whisky every morning and Mrs Merriweather, the most devout woman in Maycomb, sips gin from Lydia E Pinkham 'women's tonic' bottles. Aunt Alexandra has no secret vices, but she also has no real relationship with her husband, whom she happily leaves for an unspecified period of time, and seemingly none with her only son. Southern womanhood, the novel suggests, is not so much protected as repressed.

With both Scout's tomboyishness and Southern womanhood's unsatisfactory outcomes, the novel reaches a compromise. Scout finds something admirable in Aunt Alexandra when she sees how stoically the latter reacts to Tom's death. For the first time, Scout voluntarily takes part in one of Maycomb's feminine rituals, serving food at the missionary tea. 'After all,' she says to the reader, 'if Aunty could be a lady at a time like this, so could I'. Aunt Alexandra makes her own compromise. After Bob Ewell's attack, she dresses Scout in overalls instead of the pink dress with smocking that Scout had been wearing that night, a dress that represents the 'starched walls of a pink cotton penitentiary' that Scout fears is her fate. At the missionary tea, Scout had accidentally told the ladies that she was wearing her 'britches' under her dress, and this is exactly how she ends the novel: mid-way between tomboy and Southern lady.

To Kill a Mockingbird ultimately reaches a compromise on one of its central questions of gender: whether Scout Finch will grow up to be a Southern lady. Scout begins the novel as an unreclaimed tomboy, playing with boys, admiring men, and rejecting the pattern of womanhood that Maycomb offers her. She continues to reject the idea of whole-heartedly adopting this pattern, as the novel shows the repression and secret vices beneath the powder and pretty dresses. But Scout does not remain only a tomboy. By the end of the novel, both Scout and *To Kill a Mockingbird* have come to recognise that Southern womanhood may have its virtues as well as its vices.

REFERENCES & READING

Text

Lee, Harper 1960, *To Kill a Mockingbird*, Arrow Books, London.

Other references

Crespino, Joseph 2000, 'The strange career of Atticus Finch', *Southern Cultures*, Vol 6, no 2, pp.9–29.

Freedman, Monroe H 1994, 'Atticus Finch – right and wrong', *Alabama Law Review*, Vol 45, pp.473–82.

Garton, Stephen 2003, 'Managing mercy: African-Americans, parole and paternalism in the Georgia prison system 1919–1945', *Journal of Social History*, Vol 36, no 3, pp.675–699.

Johnson, Claudia Durst 1994, *To Kill a Mockingbird: Threatening Boundaries*, Twayne's Masterwork Studies 139, Twayne, New York.

Lay, Shawn, ed 2004, *The Invisible Empire in the West: Towards a New Historical Appraisal of the Ku Klux Klan in the 1920s*, University of Illinois Press, 2004.

Litwack, Leon F. 2009, *How Free is Free? The Long Death of Jim Crow* (Nathan I. Huggins Lectures), Harvard University Press, Cambridge, MA.

Lubet, Steven 1999, 'Reconstructing Atticus Finch', *Michigan Law Review*, Vol 97, no 6, pp.1339–62.

MacKethan, Lucinda 2005, 'Genres of Southern literature, Southern spaces', http://www.Southernspaces.org/contents/2004/mackethan/5a.v2.htm.

Petry, Alice Hall, ed 2008, *On Harper Lee: Essays and Reflections*, University of Tennessee Press, Knoxville.

Phelps, Teresa Godwin 1994, 'The margins of Maycomb: A rereading of *To Kill a Mockingbird*,' *Alabama Law Review*, Vol 45, pp.511–30.

Seidel, Kathryn Lee 2007, 'Resisting the code for Southerners in *To Kill a Mockingbird*,' in Alice Hall Petry, ed, *On Harper Lee: Essays and Reflections*, University of Tennessee Press, Knoxville, pp.79–92.

Shields, Charles J. 2007, *Mockingbird: A Portrait of Harper Lee*, Holt Paperbacks, New York.

Staff of the Klanwatch Project, comp. 1997, *Ku Klux Klan: A History of Racism and Violence*, Southern Poverty Law Center, Montgomery, Alabama.

notes